HOT BUTTONS
on
APOLOGETICS

HOT BUTTONS

on

APOLOGETICS
The What & Why of Belief & Its Defense

by
Frank R. Shivers

LIGHTNING SOURCE
1246 Heil Quaker Blvd.
La Vergne, TN

Unless otherwise noted, Scripture quotations are from
The Holy Bible *King James Version*

Library of Congress Cataloging-in-Publication Data

Shivers, Frank R., 1949-
Hot Buttons on Apologetics / Frank Shivers
ISBN 978-1-878127-14-3

Library of Congress Control Number:
2012900128

Cover design by
Tim King of Click Graphics, Inc.

For Information:
Frank Shivers Evangelistic Association
P. O. Box 9991
Columbia, South Carolina 29290
www.frankshivers.com

To

Paul Mew, who encouraged this writing

Contents

Preface

"A skeptic is a person who would ask God for his ID card."[1]
—Edgar A. Shoaff

Do all religions pray to the same God? Sixty-three percent of teens believe they do. Do teens believe in the resurrection of Jesus from the grave? Only fifty-one percent think so. Do teens believe the Holy Spirit is a living entity? Sixty-eight percent do not. Do teens believe in the reality of Satan? Sixty-five percent don't think so. Do teens believe in the sinlessness of Jesus? Nearly half, forty-six percent, believe He sinned. Do teens believe in absolute truth? Seventy percent state there is no absolute moral truth.[2] Three out of four teens, upon departure from home, drop out of church. Such alarming statistics point out the timeliness and relevancy of this book.

In the Bible book of Ecclesiastes, an account is recorded about an old and foolish king who refused to be admonished (Ecclesiastes 4:13). He had become set in his ways and close-minded to any instruction, warning, or correction. This king became so accustomed to sanctioning as truth what *he* believed that even God could not change his mind. No wonder the Bible calls him foolish.

Sadly, many students identify with this king in refusing to be open-minded to evidence that may alter their skepticism regarding God and the Christian faith. Simply put, "Satan, who is the god of this world, has blinded the minds of those who don't believe. They are unable to see the glorious light of the Good News. They don't understand this message about the glory of Christ, who is the exact likeness of God" (2 Corinthians 4:4 NLT). For people who are such, we must pray for spiritual illumination.

Truth about God and Christianity can only be ascertained through honest investigation of biblical and nonbiblical facts, observation, and ultimately the illumination of the Holy Spirit. "True-Truth," as Francis Schaffer called it, awaits the seeker of it. The Bible promises: "But if...thou shalt seek the Lord thy God, thou shalt find him, if thou seek him with all thy heart and with all thy soul" (Deuteronomy 4: 29). "And you shall seek me, and find me, when you shall search for me with all your heart" (Jeremiah 29: 13 AKJV). "And ye shall know the truth, and the truth shall make you free" (John 8: 32).

> "To say of what is that it is not, or of what is not that it is, is false; while to say of what is that it is, and of what is not that it is not, is true."—Aristotle in *Metaphysics IV*

The task of those who know the truth (Christians) is to convey it convincingly to the unbelieving so they may be saved. Prerequisite to this is acquisition and absorption of the teachings of Christianity as taught in Holy Scripture—essentially, why you believe what you believe. *Hot Buttons on Apologetics* is written to this end. The information shared within this work is basic, intended to strengthen your faith and serve as a foundation on which to build a defense for the faith.

Walk through the pages of this book slowly, seeking to comprehend and digest the truth it proclaims so that at its end, you will not only have grown in biblical knowledge, truth, and devotion to God, but in wisdom regarding its defense.

"That thou mightest know the certainty of those things, wherein thou hast been instructed."—Luke 1:4

"A person knows Christianity is true because the Holy Spirit tells him it is true, and while argument and evidence can be used to support this conclusion, they cannot legitimately overrule it."[3]
—William Lane Craig

"Oh, the wonders [the Gospel] will accomplish! It wipes guilt from the conscience—rolls the world out of the heart and darkness from the mind;...It will put honey into the bitterest cup and health into the most diseased soul....It will give hope to the heart, health to the face, oil to the head, light to the eye, strength to the hand, and swiftness to the foot. It will make life pleasant, labor sweet, and death triumphant. It gives faith to the fearful, courage to the timid, and strength to the weak. It robs the grave of its terrors and death of its sting. It subdues sin; severs from self; makes faith strong, love active, hope lively, and zeal invincible. It gives sonship for slavery and robes for rags, makes the cross light and reproach pleasant; it will transform a dungeon into a palace and make the fires of martyrdom as refreshing as the cool breeze of summer. It snaps legal bonds, loosens the soul, clarifies the mind, purifies the affections, and often lifts the saint to the very gates Heaven. No man can deserve it; money cannot buy it or good deeds procure it. Grace reigns here!"[4]—W. Poole Balfern

Chapter 1   Understanding Apologetics

"Christianity is a FACTual religion."—Josh McDowell

"Christianity is based on indisputable facts...."[5]—D. E. Jenkins

[Apologetics: A ready verbal defense for belief; not to be confused with "apology" (to request pardon). *Apologia* (apologetics) is found eight times in the New Testament in passages like Acts 22:1 and 1 Peter 3:15. You engage in apologetics when giving answer to questions regarding the why of belief.]

Seventy-five percent of Christian students upon high school graduation leave the church.[6] That's a whopping 3 out of every 4. Why? Intellectual skepticism is the biggest contributing reason, due to a shallow or skewed or spurious theology or belief system. Unsettled in what they believe and why, teens entering young adulthood encounter liberal professors and friends that shatter their faith with questioning, reasoning and argumentation. It is more imperative than ever that students be well grounded in sound doctrinal and moral theology, "always being prepared to make a defense to anyone who asks you for a reason for the hope that is in you; yet do it with gentleness and respect" (I Peter 3: 15 ESV).

It's been said that what we win teens *with,* we win them *to.* Obviously the church is winning most of them to emotion or social functions or relationships (which I'm not denying are good in their place), when she ought to be winning them mentally or intelligently to the faith. Just because one is a Christian doesn't mean he checks his brains at the door. Students must develop a firm foundation for biblical beliefs in adolescence or sadly experience shipwreck spiritually in adulthood.

Unexpectedly one's faith will be challenged. It may come through sorrow, death, suffering, rejection, persecution, or those who are lost. It may come by way of a friend, atheist, teacher, or professor; but come it will. Always be ready for it by learning how to give a reason for what you believe so you can secure spiritual footing and win the unbeliever. As a lawyer studies rigorously to master the state legal code so he may give the best appeal to the jury to convince them of his case, just so the Christian must study to master God's Book so that a winning case may be presented to the jury of the world.

The church needs strong and sharp minds to give capable defense of the faith and mount an offense for it. Emotional reasoning for one's belief is not sufficient. The intellect must be engaged to combat the skeptics and heresies victoriously. To state "the Bible says" to some skeptics is sufficient, but for many others it is not. These want to know the grounds for the authority of the Bible and why it is to be believed. To state "Jesus is the Son of God" will cause some by faith to believe, while others demand evidence. To state "God is the Creator and sustainer of all that exists" is to present a no-brainer for many, but others will require documentation.

Either the believer can simply shrug the most brazen skeptic off, counting him as unimportant, or he can do his homework well so that he may win the skeptic to Christ. The believer's option is pointedly clear in scripture (2 Peter 3:9). Ever remember that included in Jesus' command to love the Lord God with all one's soul, heart and strength is to love Him also with all the mind (Luke 10:27). "It is the responsibility of each generation," stated Jerry Falwell, "to deliver to the next a simple, undiluted, biblically accurate definition of the everlasting Gospel of Christ."[7]

The mind is a terrible thing to waste, especially when its acquisition and absorption of knowledge philosophically, scientifically, metaphysically, historically and biblically can be the means, under the anointing of the Holy Spirit, to win skeptics to Christ. The church needs more who are evangelical intellectuals. "An intelligent Christian," writes Clark Pinnock, "ought to be able to point up the flaws in a non-Christian position and to present facts and arguments which tell in favor of the Gospel. If our apologetic prevents us from explaining the Gospel to any person, it is an inadequate apologetic."[8]

Obviously not everything in Scripture has tangible evidence, but far more does than most Christians and non-Christians imagine. It is the believer's task to study the faith so thoroughly that a presentation of evidence substantiating its claims may be convincingly and concretely made. The goal in apologetics is to convince the skeptic that the embracing of the Christian faith is not only reasonable but right. "Faith in Christianity," wrote Paul Little, "is based on evidence. It is reasonable faith. Faith in the Christian sense goes *beyond* reason, but not *against* it."[9]

"Scientific proof," writes Alex McFarland "is about repetition in a controlled environment. In other words, the scientific method can be used only to prove repeatable outcomes in controlled studies; it isn't adequate for proving or disproving many questions about a person or event in history."[10] Questions pertaining to people like George Washington, William Shakespeare and even Jesus are outside the scientific realm to prove, because people and events cannot be repeated and controlled in studies. Rather, it is legal-historical proof (exhibits, oral testimony, and written testimony) which shows beyond reasonable doubt the truth about the existence and work of such people.[11] In providing a defense for the Christian faith, it is the legal-historical proof coupled with the Bible which the apologist utilizes.

Every student with study can practice apologetics. It is neither essential nor practical to master every possible objection to the Christian faith. Just be ready for those that are likely to be encountered. In witnessing to skeptics, it is awesome to know that you are not alone. Do you recall the story of the prophet Elisha in Dothan under siege by the Syrian army (2 Kings 6:8–18)? Elijah awoke early one morning only to see the city surrounded by chariots, horses, and a host of enemy Syrian troops. Seeing all this, Elisha's servant said, "Alas, my master! how shall we do?"

Elisha responded, "Fear not: for they that be with us are more than they that be with them." The prophet then prayed for God to open the servant's eyes that he might see the grand host of chariots of fire upon the mountain that surrounded them.

Out there in the trenches, presenting the Gospel at times becomes a scary thing regarding whom we see and where we go. At such a time, remember the chariots of fire. There is no need to fear or panic, for God has encompassed you on every side with a heavenly host providing protection. You may need to pause and pray, requesting God to open your eyes to "see" them, but there they are regardless of the fact that you can't see them. In warring for souls, God backs the Christian up to the hilt! You can take that to the bank.

Excellent reference books for personal study and for skeptics to read include *The Case for a Creator*, *The Case for Christ* and *The Case for the Real Jesus* (Lee Strobel); *More Evidence That Demands a Verdict* and *Evidence for Christianity* (Josh McDowell); *I Don't Have Enough Faith to Be an Atheist* (Norman Geisler); *Mere Christianity* and *God in the Dock* (C. S. Lewis); *10 Answers for Skeptics* (Alex McFarland); *The Language of God: A Scientist Presents Evidence for Belief* (Francis Collins) and *God Doesn't Believe in Atheists* (Ray Comfort).

A secure standing in the faith, the hope of tomorrow's church, and advancement of the evangelical faith rest in major part upon Christian students' mastery of the Bible and proficiency in its defense (apologetics). The Apostle Paul's instruction to young Timothy is most timely with regard to students. "Study to shew thyself approved unto God, a workman that needeth not to be ashamed, rightly dividing the word of truth" (2 Timothy 2:15). "We should know our subject profoundly and share it simply."[12]

Hints in Confronting a Skeptic

It will avail little to talk to a person about Jesus until he or she acknowledges there is a God who had a Son. Nor will it avail much to speak of the Bible as the Word of God until a person acknowledges there is a God who has a Word. Witnessing to skeptics is like working with building blocks. In order to get the person to building block E (reception of Christ as Lord and Savior), we must first get him to acknowledge building block A (the fact of God), building block B (the fact that this God has a Word), building block C (the fact of man's sin and separation from this God), and building block D (the fact that Jesus is God's Son who lived, died, and was raised from the dead to reconcile man to God). In confronting skeptics, listen closely to ascertain which building blocks are in place, and proceed lovingly to share logical and/or biblical reasons for the next block to be added.

The apostle Paul states that the "natural man" is spiritually blinded and cannot see the truth about God and eternal verities (1 Corinthians 2:14) unless his eyes are opened supernaturally (neither you nor I can do it). The best logical and scriptural presentation to the skeptic will but fall upon deaf ears unless the Holy Spirit convicts of sin, righteousness, and judgment. The apologist therefore must earnestly intercede in prayer in the skeptic's behalf that his gospel presentation will be used by the Holy Spirit as healing "eye salve" for blinded eyes.

The building block scenario necessitates biblical and nonbiblical knowledge, which this book in some measure will present. It is essential that the Christian understand and be able to communicate the grounds for Christianity intellectually and convincingly. Couch everything in the witness in love and compassion. Alex McFarland states, "I've come to realize that effective outreach to skeptics is probably about 80 percent relationship and 20 percent persuasive evidence. With friendliness and a winsome spirit, a Christian should try to connect with the person God has placed in his path."[13]

Choke down the compulsion to be argumentative. You very well could win the argument but lose the soul. Don't cower down due to a person's elevated position, status or academic degrees. All men stand on level ground at the foot of the cross with no difference in regard to sin and the need of reconciliation to God.

How are you to handle the questions of unbelievers regarding rare objections when the answers are unknown? The Philosopher of Religion William Lane Craig answers, "If you cannot answer an unbeliever's objection at some point, admit it, and refer him to literature on the subject that can satisfy his question."[14] Additionally call in the cavalry (student minister, pastor, or other trained staff) requesting assistance in dealing with the objection raised. It's okay to say, "I don't know."

Last but certainly not least in confronting skeptics, be mindful of the mind games Satan can play seeking to unravel your faith. The Apostle Paul gives a word of great caution. "Brethren, if a man be overtaken in a fault, ye which are spiritual, restore such an one in the spirit of meekness; considering thyself, lest thou also be tempted" (Galatians 6:1). It's always time to retreat when the rescuer is being pulled under by the rescuee.

ASK YOURSELF

Define apologetics?

How many times is the word used in the New Testament?

Why is a study in apologetics needful?

What was Clark Pinnock's point?

What is the goal in apologetics?

Cite Paul Little's statement about Christianity's being a reasonable faith, and explain what he meant.

If someone asked the reason for your belief that Jesus is the only way to Heaven, how might you respond?

Memorize I Peter 3:15 and share it with a friend, or, if in a group, study it with them.

Name several hints cited for sharing with a skeptic.

Chapter 2   The Existence of God

"In the beginning God created the heaven and the earth."
—Genesis 1:1.

Beware of manufacturing a God of your own: a God who is all mercy, but not just; a God who is all love, but not holy; a God who has a Heaven for everybody, but a Hell for none; a God who can allow good and bad to be side by side in time, but will make no distinction between good and bad in eternity. Such a God is an idol of your own, as truly an idol as any snake or crocodile in an Egyptian temple. The hands of your own fancy and sentimentality have made him. He is not the God of the Bible, and beside the God of the Bible there is no God at all.[15]

There is a new breed of atheists in town—atheists who not only attack and condemn *belief in* God, but also *respect for* God. Gary Wolf stated that the New Atheists are in a "war against faith."[16] Christopher Hitchens, leader of the movement until his recent death, emphatically said that "faith should end."[17] The attack on the Christian faith by the New Atheists is now center stage on late-night talk shows, university campuses, bookstore shelves and the Internet.

The Christian faith can well handle all such assaults, but sadly believers who are unfounded in the theological, historical, and scientific reasons for belief in God often cannot handle them. It is more imperative than ever to heed Peter's admonition: "But respect Christ as the holy Lord in your hearts. Always be ready to answer everyone who asks you to explain about the hope you have, but answer in a gentle way and with respect" (I Peter 3:15–16 NCV). A simple understanding of the basics of the faith learned in Sunday school or at church camp will not suffice to fend off the attack from such groups as the New Atheists. A study in Christian apologetics is essential to deepen the understanding of the doctrines of the faith and how to defend them successfully.

The Cause and Effect Argument for the Existence of God

This reason is based on the truth that for every effect there has to be a cause. There has to be an explanation for all that exists; nothing just exists. It follows to say that if there is a cause for all that exists, then there has to be a "first cause" to set things in motion. "If there is no First Cause, then the universe is like a railroad train moving without an engine. Each car's motion is explained, proximately, by the motion of the car in front of it. The caboose moves because the boxcar pulls it; the boxcar moves because the cattle car pulls it, etc. But there's no engine to pull the first car, and thus the whole train. That would be impossible, of course. But that's what the universe is like if there is no *First Cause*. Dependent beings cannot cause themselves. They are dependent on their causes. If there's no Independent Being, then the whole chain of dependent beings is dependent on nothing and could not exist. But they do exist. Therefore, there is an Independent Being."[18]

This "first cause" is God. He is the originating "domino" (Creator) that has set the world in motion.

David declared in Psalm 90:2, "Before the mountains were born or you brought forth the earth and the world, from everlasting to everlasting you are God" (NIV). Nehemiah stated, "You alone are the LORD. You made the heavens, even the highest heavens, and all their starry host, the earth and all that is on it, the seas and all that is in them. You give life to everything, and the multitudes of heaven worship you" (Nehemiah 9:6 NIV).

The Design and Designer Argument

The primal premise of this argument for the existence of God is that where there is "design," there must be a "designer." The possibility of all the intrinsic parts of a watch just coming together for its formation and accurate function is so far out that it is absurd to consider. The same applies to the intrinsic design and function of the universe. Where there is a watch, there is a watchmaker; and behind the awesome, complex universe is a master designer who is God. Physicist Paul Davies said, "There is for me powerful evidence that there is something going on behind it all....It seems as though somebody has fine tuned nature's numbers to make the universe....The impression of design is overwhelming."[19] Upon examination of the human body and nature, one comes to the same conclusion as the psalmist, who declared, "I praise you because I am fearfully and wonderfully made; your works are wonderful, I know that full well" (Psalm 139:14 NIV).

The Complexity of the Universe and Man

The Moon

"The moon has had other beneficial effects on the earth. Scientists now know that the earth originally had a rotational period of eight hours. Such a rapid rotational period would have resulted in surface wind velocities in excess of 500 miles per hour. The gravitational tug of the moon...has reduced the rotation period of the earth to 24 hours. Likewise, the gravitational attraction of the earth on the moon has reduced its rotational period to 29 days. Needless to say, winds of 500 miles per hour would not be conducive to the existence of higher life forms (coincidence or design?)."[20] The moon creates essential oceanic water tides and movement restraining the oceans from consuming the earth.

The Earth

The earth is just the right size—any smaller, an atmosphere would be impossible, like Mercury; any larger, its atmosphere would contain free hydrogen, like Jupiter. Earth is the only known planet to possess the right combination of gases in its atmosphere to sustain animal, plant and human life. Earth is the perfect distance from the sun. The planets just on either side of earth, Venus and Mars, are too close to the sun and too far from the sun, respectively, to support life as we see it on earth. Earth's faithful rotation on its axis enables it to be properly warmed and cooled

11

each day. The uniformity and stability of nature is another mirror revealing the hand of intelligent design of the earth. Nature operates by inert, unchanging laws. The earth rotates the same distance every 24 hours, the speed of light is consistent, gravity remains the same, and day and night do not cease. Richard Feynman, a Nobel Prize winner for quantum electrodynamics, said, "Why nature is mathematical is a mystery....The fact that there are rules at all is a kind of miracle."[21]

Water

Man's body consists mostly of water, and it needs water for its survival. Since ninety-seven percent of the earth's water is in the oceans, how is it that the pure water (free from salt) needed for the body is available? The Designer of the Universe provided that through the process of evaporation, water (without the salt) would be drawn up from the oceans, forming free-moving clouds that would scatter across the earth, dispersing water to sustain every living thing. It is a system of recycled and used water (purification) that sustains the planet.

The Eye

The design of the eye is far superior to the best lenses of photographic cameras; its automatic focusing is incomparable. The eye is able to handle 1.5 million messages at the same moment and distinguish from among 7 million colors.[22]

The Brain

The brain processes more than a million messages a second through a screening function allowing you to focus on the important and ignore the unimportant. The brain is the only organ with intelligence for decision making, emotions, planning and knowledge. Automatically, the brain controls breathing, blood pressure, heart rate, and balance to stand, walk, and run while concentrating on something else.[23]

The Heart

Dr. Phillip Bishop, professor of exercise physiology at the University of Alabama, stated: "The heart of man, from a functional viewpoint, is a miracle of performance. Through a complex nervous and hormonal feedback regulation system, the heart and circulatory systems maintain the exactly correct rate and output to supply the correct blood flow for both the marathoner and the couch potato. The parts of you that are functioning at any particular time receive a share of blood in proportion to their need, and those that are resting quietly receive their carefully metered due."[24] Such precision operation of the heart didn't happen just by chance; God designed it that way. The circulatory system of arteries, veins, and capillaries stretch about 60,000 miles, and the heart beats in excess of 2.5 billion times in an average lifetime (93,000 times per day; 655,000 times per week, 34 million times per year).

The DNA Code

In every cell of the body, there resides a detailed instruction code similar to a miniature computer program.[25] A computer program is made up of ones and zeros like this: 110010101011000; the arrangement of the numbers tells the computer its function. The DNA code (four chemicals that scientists abbreviate as A, T, G, and C) in each of our cells operate similarly and is arranged in each cell as CGTGTGACTCGCTCCTGAT, and so on. "There are three billion of these letters in EACH human cell. DNA is a three-billion-lettered program telling the cell to act in a certain way. It is a full instruction manual. These are not just chemicals. These are chemicals that instruct, that code in a very detailed way exactly how the person's body should develop."[26] Who programmed the DNA instruction manual in man? The only reasonable answer to this question is an Intelligent Designer.

Molecules

"The truth is that the simplest living cell has over one trillion molecules in it. That is more than 1,000 times 1,000 times 1,000 times 1,000 or 1,000 times one billion. All of the molecules in that cell have to be in just the right place at the right time, or the cell will either malfunction or not function and die. Think of it this way; there are from 500 to over 1,000 times more molecules in the simplest cell than there are people on Earth and, unlike the people on Earth, all of the molecules must be in exactly the right place at the right time or it won't work."[27]

Blood Cells

The body consists of 100 trillion cells, about 1 billion of which are replaced each hour. Each square inch of the body has around 19 million skin cells.

The "red blood cells, which 'incidentally' happen to be the ideal shape for transporting oxygen, are manufactured and destroyed at an incredible rate. Approximately 10 million red blood cells are made every hour, and an equal number destroyed. If either supply or destruction becomes out of synchrony by as little as 1%, before long, your life ends due to anemia or polycythemia; which is to say, your blood gets so thin than oxygen transport is insufficient, or it gets so thick that it can no longer circulate."[28]

Kidneys, Liver and Digestive Tract

The complex function of the kidneys in cleansing the blood, the liver's detoxifying of the blood, and its 500 plus vital functions and the digestive system point to the Creator God.

It is abundantly clear to see intelligent design in the makeup of the moon, sun, water, and the earth in the universe, and in the eyes, brain, heart, molecular structure, DNA, cells, liver, kidney and digestive tract of man. The law of causality states that the effect cannot be greater than the cause; if the effect is obvious intelligent design, then the cause must be one of intellect (God).

The Miracle of the Newborn Infant in the Womb
Reveals a Divine Designer

"Consider the single fertilized cell of a newly conceived human life. From that one cell within the womb develop all the different kinds of tissues, organs, and systems, all working together at just the right time in an amazingly coordinated process. An example is the hole in the septum between the two ventricles in the heart of the newborn infant. This hole closes up at exactly the right time during the birth process to allow for the oxygenation of the blood from the lungs, which does not occur while the baby is in the womb and is receiving oxygen through the umbilical cord."[29]

The Bible Confirms the Existence of God

Biblical writers did not endeavor to prove the existence of God. To them that was self-evident. However, the Bible's amazing unity, historical accuracy, archeological finds and personal testimonies of millions regarding its trustworthiness give proof to the existence of its Author, God. Evidences for the divine inspiration of the Bible and God as its Author are discussed in Hot Buttons 4–7.

The Resurrection of Christ Proves God's Existence

God appeared to man robed in human flesh in the person of Jesus Christ. John stated, "The Word became a human and lived among us. We saw his glory—the glory that belongs to the only Son of the Father—and he was full of grace and truth" (John 1:14, NCV). That the Word was God is clearly documented in Scripture: "In the beginning was the Word, and the Word was with God, and the Word was God" (John 1:1). To know what God is like, all one needs to do is look at Jesus Christ—"No one has ever seen God. But the unique One [Jesus Christ], who is himself God, is near to the Father's heart. He has revealed God to us" (John 1:18, NLT). Sin prevented man's upward reach to God, so God descended to man

15

to provide means of imperative reconciliation to Himself through death upon a Cross and resurrection three days later. Jesus Christ, in rising from the dead, validated His claim as God. The body of Jesus was buried and sealed in the tomb of Joseph and guarded by Roman soldiers (Matthew 27:65). On the third day (Easter morning), the stone was rolled away by God, and Jesus was raised from the dead (Luke 24:6). The evidence for Jesus' resurrection will be dealt with in Hot Button #3.

Max Planck, a Nobel Prize-winning physicist considered to be the founder of quantum theory and one of the most important physicists of the twentieth century, stated "Both religion and science require a belief in God. For believers, God is in the beginning; and for physicists, He is at the end of all considerations....To the former, He is the foundation; to the latter, the crown of the edifice of every generalized world view."[30]

Sir Isaac Newton, who is often regarded as the greatest scientist of all time and was himself a Christian believer, said, "God created everything by number, weight and measure."[31]

He said further, "Atheism is so senseless and odious to mankind that it never had many professors....Whence arises this uniformity in all [creatures'] outward shapes but from the counsel and contrivance of an Author?...These and such like considerations always have and ever will prevail with mankind to believe that there is a Being who made all things and has all things in His power and who is therefore to be feared."[32]

The question was asked, "Many prominent scientists—including Darwin, Einstein, and Planck—have considered the concept of God very seriously; what are your thoughts on the concept of God and on the existence of God?" Christian Anfinsen (Nobel Prize-winning chemist) replied, "I think only an idiot can be an atheist. We must admit that there exists an incomprehensible power or force with limitless foresight and knowledge that started the whole universe going in the first place."[33] Phillip E. Johnson stated, "It is really true that atheism requires gobs of blind faith, while the path of logic and reason leads straight to the Gospel of Jesus Christ."[34] C. S. Lewis said he remembered, "...night after night, feeling whenever my mind lifted even for a second from my work, the steady, unrelenting approach of Him whom I so earnestly desired not to meet. I gave in and admitted that God was God and knelt and prayed—perhaps, that night, the most dejected and reluctant convert in all of England."[35] Lewis' journey from atheist to "reluctant convert" to Christian apologist and famed writer showcases the reality of God.

"Atheism never composed a symphony, never painted a masterpiece, never dispelled a fear, never healed a disease, never gave peace of mind, never dried a tear, never established a philanthropy, never gave an intelligent answer to the vast mystery of the universe, never gave meaning to man's life on earth, never built a just and peaceful world, never built a great and enduring civilization."[36] But belief in and commitment to God has.

Having examined with open mind all that has been said, hopefully your faith has been sustained and strengthened and knowledge has been gained to withstand the fiery darts of deception and lies yet to be hurled upon it regarding God's reality.

ASK YOURSELF

Has an atheistic or agnostic professor, teacher or friend challenged your faith in God?

What do you count to be the biggest reasons for the existence of God?

How might these reasons be used in giving a defense for your faith?

Explain the "first cause" explanation for the existence of God.

Do you agree or disagree with Christian Anfinsen's assertion that only "an idiot can be an atheist?" Why or why not?

What proof does the Bible give for the existence of God and the resurrection of Christ?

What is the alternative to a belief in God?

Is atheism/agnosticism man's default condition?

Read one or more of the following books on Christian apologetics: *More Evidence That Demands a Verdict* by Josh McDowell; *Created in God's Image* by Anthony A. Hoekema; *The Case for a Creator* by Lee Strobel; *Reasonable Faith* by William Lane Craig; *Twenty Compelling Evidences That God Exists* by Kenneth Boa and Robert Bowman.

Chapter 3   The Resurrection of Jesus
"He is not here: for he is risen, as he said."—Matthew 28: 6.

"There exists such overwhelming evidence...that no intelligent jury in the world could fail to bring a verdict that the resurrection story is true."[37]—Lord Darling, former Chief Justice of England

Did Jesus actually exist? Proof of one's existence in antiquity obviously was not provided by DNA, as it might be today, but by documentation of historians. "There are at least 39 sources outside of the Bible (e.g. Flavius Josephus; Cornelius Tacitus; Thallus) within 150 years of Jesus' life that reveal more than 100 facts about His life, teachings, death, and resurrection."[38] Flavius Josephus, Jewish historian who was born in A.D. 37, stated:

"Now there was about this time Jesus, a wise man, if it be lawful to call Him a man, for He was a doer of wonderful works, a teacher of such men as receive the truth with pleasure. He drew over to Him both many of the Jews and many of the Gentiles. He was the Christ; and when Pilate, at the suggestion of the principal men among us, had condemned Him to the cross, those who loved Him at the first did not forsake Him, for He appeared to them alive again in the third day, as the divine prophets had foretold these and ten thousand other wonderful things concerning Him. And the tribe of Christians, so named from Him, are not extinct at this day."[39]

Also, "Roman government officials such as Pliny the Younger and even two Caesars, Trajan and Hadrian, wrote intriguing letters mentioning Jesus and early Christian origins. About A.D. 112, Pliny describes weekly gatherings of early Christians who met before dawn, singing and worshipping Christ as Deity."[40]

Pliny ordered every Christian who failed to deny Christ and refused to worship the gods and emperor to be put to death. Pliny's writings refer to Christians who refused this order consenting to death rather than renounce Christ.

Credible evidence for the miracles of Christ outside the Bible reveals the reality of the Christ of the Bible.

The liberal twentieth-century German theologian Rudolph Bultmann, whose approach of "demythologizing" Jesus called on people to focus more on faith instead of historical facts, said, "Of course the doubt as to whether Jesus really existed is unfounded and not worth refutation. No sane person can doubt that Jesus stands as the founder behind the historical movement whose first distinct stage is represented by the oldest Palestinian community."[41]

Recently, archeologists found a mosaic bearing the name of Jesus Christ in Megiddo along with images of a fish, an ancient Christian symbol which dates back to the third or fourth centuries.[42] The existence of Jesus was virtually unquestionable until the end of the nineteenth century, which in itself speaks loudly for His life. The historical evidence, apart from the overwhelming biblical evidence, gives indisputable proof that Jesus actually existed. With the fact of Jesus' life clearly established, how about the fact of His resurrection?

Jesus personally attested that the one eternal proof of His deity would be His resurrection from the dead (Matthew 12:39–40). Did Jesus literally rise from the dead as the Christian faith advocates, giving validation to the claim that He indeed is the Son of God? Opponents to Christianity say no. Why do they object to Jesus' resurrection, and how might their objections be silenced?

Skeptic Objections to the Resurrection of Jesus

The Stolen Body Theory

Some disbelievers of the resurrection suggest that the body of Jesus was secretly stolen from the tomb by the disciples. This theory was circulated immediately following Jesus' burial (Matthew 27:64; 28:13) and refuted by the fact that Jesus' body was heavily guarded (Matthew 27:65–66).

The Swoon Theory

This assertion says that Jesus was not dead when sealed in the tomb, but in a state of unconsciousness, and that the cool air within the tomb revived Him. However, Scripture makes it clear that Jesus was dead to the satisfaction of trained Roman soldiers. An added confirmation of this fact is that a spear pierced His side prior to removal from the cross (John 19: 34).

Hallucination Theory

This view states that Jesus did not really rise from the dead; people just hallucinated that He did. A ghostlike apparition cannot be touched, yet Thomas was invited by Jesus to place his finger in His hands and put his hand into His spear-pierced side (John 20:24–29). It is implausible to believe that so many who claimed to see the risen Christ in different places and at different times over a period of forty days all were hallucinating.

The Mistaken Tomb Theory

Advocates of this belief contend that Mary and the disciples went to the wrong tomb, a tomb that happened to be empty. If this were the case, then the Roman soldiers and Pharisees could have easily disproved the resurrection of Christ by going to the right tomb and presenting Jesus' body. Additionally, all that was necessary to prove the disciples went to the wrong tomb was to ask Joseph, the owner of the tomb in which Jesus was buried. He could have solved the problem instantly.

Internal and External Attestations to the Resurrection of Christ

The Soldiers

Roman soldiers (elite trained fighting men of the highest order) guarded Jesus' tomb to insure a resurrection hoax couldn't be fabricated. How many soldiers were stationed at the tomb? Possibly more than sixteen, for that was the number that guarded

21

Peter when he was imprisoned. One would think the Romans would certainly guard Jesus' tomb with more care than they guarded Peter. These soldiers, under the sentence of death by torture should Jesus' body be stolen, certainly would not have fallen asleep and allowed that to occur (Matthew 27:62–66).

The Stone

The stone that sealed Jesus' tomb weighed one and a half to two tons (approximate weight of a mid-size car)—far too huge for a few men to roll away at all, and certainly not without awakening the soldiers, had they fallen asleep (Matthew 27:66).

The Seal

The Roman Seal, which stood for the power and authority of the Roman Empire, was affixed to the tomb. Automatic execution by crucifixion upside down would be the lot of anyone who broke the seal. Who would risk such a horrible death for a prank?

The Site

Jesus' tomb was near Jerusalem (John 19:42) where His resurrection was first announced. No doubt there were some "doubting Thomases" who went to the tomb to see for themselves. Had Christ not been raised from the dead, the claim that He had would not have lasted an hour. Jewish and Roman sources (ranging from Josephus to a compilation of fifth-century Jewish writings called the *Toledoth Jeshu)* stipulate the tomb was empty. [43]

The Shroud

The linen wrappings that had been placed on the body of Jesus were found in the tomb in a fashion that indicated Jesus simply passed through them. Obviously had thieves taken Jesus' body, these wrappings would have been in disarray.

The Sightings

The next forty days following the resurrection, Jesus revealed Himself to over 1,500 people before returning to Heaven (1 Corinthians 15:3–6). British theologian Michael Green states, "The appearances of Jesus are as well authenticated as anything in antiquity....There can be no rational doubt that they occurred."[44]

Christ appeared to:

• Mary Magdalene (John 20:11–18);

• Other women (Matthew 28:9, 10);

• Two disciples on the Emmaus Road (Luke 24:13–35);

• Ten disciples (John 20:19–25);

• Thomas (John 20:26–31);

• Seven disciples on the Sea of Galilee (John 21:1–25);

• The eleven disciples at the giving of the Great Commission (Matthew 28:16–20);

• The five hundred [only men were numbered in New Testament times; factoring in women and children, this number could easily have exceeded 1,500] (1 Corinthians 15:6);

• Those at His ascension (Acts 1:9–10);

• Paul (Acts 9:3–6);

• John (Revelation 1:10–18)

• James (1 Corinthians 15:7)

• Peter (1 Corinthians 15:5)

• The disciples without Thomas (John 20:26)

• The eleven disciples in the upper room (Luke 24:36)

Lee Strobel, in *The Case for the Real Jesus,* states that a significant proof of Christ's resurrection lies in the fact that the early New Testament accounts of the resurrection were written during the lifetime of many who witnessed or heard of it. This timeline assured eyewitness documentation (accurate, fresh) of the resurrection and provided disbelievers the opportunity to rebut it had it not been true—but none did.[45]

The Saints

Another evidence of Christ's resurrection is in the change that was manifested in the disciples. Prior to it, they were fearful and cowardly, but after seeing the risen Christ, they were bold and courageous in proclaiming the Gospel. The disciples would not have suffered and died (eleven of the twelve died a martyr's death) for a known hoax. People don't die for what they know is a lie.

Paul's conversion from being anti-Christ to being a follower of Christ, from being a persecutor of the saints to being a praiser of Christ, occurred after the resurrection. Seeing the risen Christ on the Damascus Road, Paul was convinced of His resurrection and claim as being the Son of God to the degree that his life forever was changed from that moment forward. Thousands of people converted to Christ immediately after His resurrection, something that never would have happened had they not been convinced that He, in fact, had risen from the grave (Acts 2:41; 4:33). The testimonies of multitudes of saints through the years who had previously been atheists, agnostics, drunkards, drug addicts or had been ensnared deeply in some other sin verify that Jesus lives through the transformation He has wrought in their lives.

The Sibling

The historian Josephus refers to the half-brother of Jesus whose name was James, as do both Mark and John in Scripture (Mark 3:21, 31; 6:3–4; John 7:3–5). James was not a believer until Jesus appeared unto Him following His resurrection (1 Corinthians

15:7). "As a result of his encounter with the risen Jesus," Michael Licona states, "James doesn't just become a Christian, but he later becomes leader of the Jerusalem church. Actually, James was so thoroughly convinced of Jesus' Messiahship because of the resurrection that he died as a martyr, as both Christian and non-Christian sources attest."[46]

Lee Strobel asked Licona, "In the end, do you think James' conversion is significant evidence for the resurrection?"

He stated frankly, "Absolutely, yes, I do."[47]

The Sabbath

The resurrection of Christ was so believed by the early church that they engaged in corporate worship on Sunday to celebrate it—something the Christian church yet does. "And upon the first day of the week, when the disciples came together to break bread, Paul preached unto them, ready to depart on the morrow; and continued his speech until midnight" (Acts 20:7). The Sabbath was part of the Old Testament covenant associated with the Lawgiver; the first day of the week is part of the New Covenant associated with the Grace-Giver, Jesus Christ. This covenant is based on the life, death and resurrection to provide man the means of reconciliation to God.

ASK YOURSELF

What historical evidence is there for the existence of Jesus?

Why is the resurrection of Christ important?

Why do you believe that Jesus was raised from the dead?

What might you say to a person who does not accept the resurrection of Jesus?

What is the Christian's response to the four theories objecting to the resurrection of Christ?

To you, what is the strongest evidence for the resurrection of Jesus?

Why do you think James remained an unbeliever until after seeing the risen Christ?

Do you know others whose skepticism overshadows the truth about Jesus?

Chapter 4   Can the Bible Be Trusted?
Archeology Answers

"All scripture is given by inspiration of God, and is profitable for doctrine, for reproof, for correction, for instruction in righteousness."—2 Timothy 3: 16.

It is no mere Book. It is a living creature. It conquers all who fight it.[48]—Napoleon

There is no other book like the Bible. The Bible [from the Latin *biblia* (books)] is God's only written revelation to man. The Bible "is a vast library," states R. G. Lee, "in one volume, written by forty men of different capacity and temperament and position over a period of 1,600 years; [it] has one message—progressive, constructive, complete."[49] It contains 66 books—39 in the Old Testament (before Christ) and 27 in the New Testament (beginning with the story of Christ). The text of the Bible is itself a well-documented piece of antiquity.

Totally true in fact and doctrine, the Bible contains no contradictions and is thoroughly trustworthy. "Through the Holy Spirit's agency, God is involved in both the production and interpretation of Scripture. Men of God in antiquity spoke as they were moved by the Holy Spirit. 'Moved' means literally 'to bear along.' Scripture is infallible precisely because the Holy Spirit 'bore along' the prophets who spoke and wrote"[50] (2 Peter 1:20–21). The Bible is not simply to be believed; it is to be applied to one's life (James 1:22).

While the Bible validates itself through an array of internal supports of its reliability—consistency, multiple witnesses, verifiable history—the Bible is also validated by many external evidences. For instance, it has been confirmed by more than one hundred archeological finds. To mention a few:

• At one time, scholars denied as factual the existence and description of the Hittite nation, until their capital and records were discovered at Bogazkoy, Turkey.[51]

- Skeptics thought Solomon's wealth was greatly exaggerated until recent discoveries revealed that wealth in antiquity was concentrated with the king.[52]

- Some claimed that there was never an Assyrian king named Sargon (Isaiah 20:1) until his palace was discovered in Khorsabad, Iraq.[53]

- King Belshazzar (Daniel 5) also was counted to be fictitious, until tablets were found showing that he was Nabonidus' son who served as coregent in Babylon.[54]

- Outside the Bible, no documentation was known to give credence to the existence of Pontius Pilate. But in 1961, archeologists discovered at Caesarea a stone inscription that bore Pontius Pilate's inscription honoring the Roman emperor Tiberius. Coins have also been discovered dating from Pilate's gubernatorial rule.[55]

- Ruins of the synagogue at Capernaum, where Jesus taught, and of Peter's house in Capernaum have been discovered. Archeological evidence for the existence of Paul has been validated overwhelmingly by ruins in Cyprus, Galatia, Philippi, Thessalonica, Berea, Athens, Corinth, Ephesus, Rome, and surrounding areas. The rule of Herod the Great at the time of Jesus' birth is substantiated by the numerous excavations of his massive public works in the Holy Land, including the Great Temple in Jerusalem.[56]

Dead Sea Scrolls

A young Palestinian boy on February 20, 1947, while tending some flocks in the Qumran area of Israel, decided to explore some caves. In one of the caves, he discovered old clay pots containing scrolls of books in the Old Testament. Further investigations in this same area led to the recovery of documents from eleven additional caves. In excess of eight hundred documents were discovered which contained complete and incomplete scrolls of the entire Old Testament text except Esther, scrolls that date back to one hundred years before Christ. The Isaiah scroll is over a thousand years old. The Dead Sea Scrolls of the Old Testament text are older by at least a thousand years than any other Hebrew text of the Old Testament known to be in existence until its discovery.[57] The archeological discovery of the Dead Sea Scrolls, the greatest in the twentieth century, substantiates the integrity and accuracy of Scripture.

The House of David Inscription

Scholars who refuted that King David ever lived had reason to change their minds on July 21, 1993, when an inscribed stone was discovered at the base of Mount Hermon in Israel which mentioned King David's dynasty.

Declared R. G. Lee: "The accuracy of its [Bible] statements and prophecies is substantiated by every turn of the excavator's spade in Bible lands, by history, by multitudinous inscriptions deciphered among classic ruins by the unlocking of Egyptian hieroglyphics. From rusty coins and corroded marbles, we find confirmations of its own veracity."[58]

"There is no event in ancient history that can produce more than a fraction of evidence by which the Bible in its entirety is sustained as genuine and authentic. The Christian has more proof and more right to believe that all the versions of Scripture had one original than for Americans to believe that all the copies of the Declaration of Independence had one original."[59]

The archeologist's blade is ever confirming the Bible as truth and will continue to do so until the return of Christ. While some people like to doubt the authenticity of the Bible, they ignore the historical fact that it is better documented than any other ancient writing that most people take for granted as authentic. The biblical text is better preserved and more thoroughly supported by scholarly evidence, for instance, than the writings of Plato and Aristotle. Charles Ryrie states, "More than 5,000 manuscripts of the New Testament exist today, which makes the New Testament the best-attested document of all ancient writings."[60] Josh McDowell notes, "Compared with other ancient writings, the Bible has more manuscript evidence to support it than any ten pieces of classical literature combined."[61] While archeological evidence proves that the people, places and events of the Bible are real, a person yet has to exhibit faith with regard to its spiritual message—man, due to sin, is separated from God and may only be reconciled to Him through a personal relationship with His Son, the Lord Jesus Christ.

Thomas Newberry (author of the Newberry Bible) just prior to his death was asked if he had ever been tormented with doubts as to the inspiration of the Bible. He replied, "I have spent sixty years in the study of the Scriptures in the original languages, marking carefully every tense and preposition, and the impression left on my mind is not the difficulty of believing but the impossibility of doubting the inspiration of the Scriptures."[62] All who make a study of it hold the same belief.

ASK YOURSELF

How convincing is biblical archeology for believing the Bible?

To a skeptical world, is such evidence acceptable? Why or why not?

The rich man in Luke 16:27–31 asked that someone from the dead be sent to warn his brothers of the reality of Hell. What was Abraham's reply? Why?

Relate this to a person who desires more and more archeological discoveries to validate the Bible before he accepts it as God's Word.

In what way is the Bible better documented than any other ancient writing?

What is the significance of the Dead Sea Scrolls?

Chapter 5   Why Believe the Bible?
Prophecy Answers

"And he said unto them, These are the words which I spake unto you, while I was yet with you, that all things must be fulfilled, which were written in the law of Moses, and in the prophets, and in the psalms, concerning me."—Luke 24: 44.

Prophetic evidence validates the Holy Bible as true. "Fulfilled prophecy," states John MacArthur, "is perhaps the greatest proof that the Word of God is true. It carries the weight of proof for the Word of God further than any other single element of Scripture."[63]

Prophecy Regarding Christ

"How many people would it take flipping a quarter before one person hits heads thirty times in a row? According to *Ripley's Believe It or Not! Strange Coincidences*, 'In order for a coin to land on heads fifty times in a row, it would take one million men flipping ten coins a minute, forty hours a week; and then it would happen only once every nine hundred years.' There are at least thirty prophecies about the birth, the death, and the resurrection of the Messiah that were fulfilled in Jesus Christ. Wouldn't you agree that's a whole lot like tossing a coin thirty times in a row and having it come up heads?"[64] Declared Norman Geisler, "All the evidence points to Jesus as the divinely appointed fulfillment of the Messianic prophecies. He was God's Man, confirmed by God's signs."[65]

Micah prophesied the place where Jesus would be born, in Bethlehem Ephratah (Micah 5:2), and He *was* born there—700 years later. Isaiah prophesied Jesus would be born of a virgin (Isaiah 7:14), and He was. Daniel prophesied the exact year that Jesus would die (Daniel 9:24–27), and He died precisely at that time. How can this be known? Daniel predicted that in sixty-nine weeks—sixty-nine sevens of years, or 483 years—Christ would die. Nehemiah informs us that the date of this decree by Artaxerxes was the twentieth year of his reign (Nehemiah 2:1). Exactly 483 years from the time of that decree lands us at Calvary when Jesus died. Isaiah prophesied hundreds of years prior to Jesus' birth that He would be buried with the rich (Isaiah 53:9). This was fulfilled, despite the fact that Jesus was poor. He was buried in the unused tomb of a wealthy man, something unheard of prior to this. The same prophecy declared that Jesus would die with the wicked, something that indeed happened when He was crucified between two thieves. Jeremiah prophesied that the Messiah would be a descendant of King David (Jeremiah 23:5–6). Jesus was, according to Matthew 1. Isaiah foretold the rejection of Christ by His unbelieving people (Isaiah 53). This prophecy was fulfilled (John 1:11).

In sharing the probability of just eight prophecies about the Messiah—His place of birth, time of birth, manner of birth, betrayal, manner of death, reaction to death (mocking, spitting), side being pierced and burial—being fulfilled in any one man, Peter Stoner stated, "We find that the chance that any man might have lived down to the present time and fulfilled all eight prophecies is 1 in 10 to the 17th power. That would be 1 in 100,000,000,000,000,000." Stoner illustrates. Suppose, he says, that 10 to the 17th power of silver dollars (with only one marked) were laid all over Texas, covering the state two feet deep, then stirred thoroughly. Now, he continues, have a blindfolded man travel as far across Texas as he wants in search of the one marked silver dollar. What is the likelihood of this blindfolded man picking up the right silver dollar? Stoner states it would be the same chance that the prophets would have had of writing these eight prophecies and having them all come true in any one man, from their day to the present time, providing they wrote them according to their own wisdom.[66] Yet Jesus fulfilled them all. This adds credible evidence that the Bible is what it claims to be, the inspired Word of God.

"On one single day of twenty-four hours," states John Linton, "from the time of Christ's arrest in Gethsemane to the hour when He was buried in the shadow of the cross, no less than half a hundred specific prophecies were fulfilled! Any mathematician will tell you that the numerical chance of accidental fulfillment would run into astronomical figures against it. Just to mention a few, four classes of people were to be active in the crucifixion (Psalm 2:1–2). Christ was to be sold for silver, betrayed by a friend, forsaken by disciples. The betrayer would eat bread at a table with Him. His hands and feet would be pierced. He would drink vinegar and gall. They would cast lots for His vesture. The price of betrayal would go to the potter's field. What of those prophecies? Were they fulfilled? They were fulfilled…accurately."[67]

Daniel's Prophecy

Skeptics attack the book of Daniel constantly because he proves the inspiration of the Bible by foretelling 2,500 years of history. One can only deny its divine inspiration by saying Daniel was written after the facts. But such belief is absurd and foolish, for much of what Daniel prophesied had not occurred during Jesus' time on earth (Matthew 24:15).[68]

ASK YOURSELF

How does biblical prophecy substantiate the claim that the Bible is true?

How strong an argument for the Bible does Peter Stoner give?

Coupling archeological evidence with the prophetic, what is your view of Scripture?

Complete the following statement: "I believe the Bible is God's Word because..."

What evidence for divine inspiration of the Bible is found in the book of Daniel?

Chapter 6   Is the Bible Credible?
Science Answers
"It is in truth, the word of God."—I Thessalonians 2:13.

"A little science estranges a man from God; a lot of science brings him back."[69]—Francis Bacon

The Bible contains scientific facts that were not known to man for hundreds of years. How could that be? It was divinely authored by an all-knowing God. These scientific facts clearly give credence to the authority of the Bible. "The Bible," states John R. Rice, "is a book of science. It plainly deals with many scientific matters. And whenever the Bible mentions matters of science, it does it with the absolute authority of the infallible Word of God. God made the world, and God made the Bible. So when God speaks in the Bible about the world He made, He tells the exact truth."[70]

Science Validates the Bible

The Stars

The great mathematicians and astronomers, Hipparchus (190 B.C.) and Ptolemy (A.D. 90) studied the stars. The first stated there were 1,022 stars, and the second, 1,026 stars. But Moses in the Bible stated fourteen hundred years before Christ that they were innumerable (Genesis 15:5).[71] The prophet Jeremiah, under inspiration of the Holy Spirit, said, "The host of heaven cannot be numbered" (33:22). How did Moses and Jeremiah know the starry host was innumerable centuries before the birth of Christ, when learned men did not know until nearly 2,000 years later? God told them.

The Empty Space in the North Skies

Scientists studying the stars have been puzzled in noting their vast array in every direction but the north. In the northern skies, there is an empty space. God told mankind about this empty space fifteen hundred years before Christ.[72] Job penned under inspiration, "He [God] stretcheth out the north over the empty place" (Job 26:7).

The Moon

For centuries men believed the moon was an orb like the sun, but dim due to age. Man had it all wrong and would have known so had he read Job 25:5, "The moon...it shineth not"!

The Earth Floats Freely in Space

Strangely, people in antiquity believed the earth set upon the back of a turtle or elephant or was upheld by Atlas.[73] But Job, during that time, wrote that He "hangeth the earth upon nothing" (Job 26:7). No other writer of antiquity declared such. How did Job know the world was suspended upon nothing when the bright minds of the day did not? God told him!

The Earth Is Round

Many believed that if Columbus sailed far enough, he would drop off the earth into a great abyss. The belief that the earth was not round perpetuated this belief. But God clearly declared in His Book that the earth was round. "It is he that sitteth upon the circle [literally, "roundness"] of the earth" (Isaiah 40:22). Isaiah clearly knew long before astrologers that the earth was not flat, but spherical.

The Earth's Rotation

Centuries ago, men believed that the sun circled the earth in twenty-four hour cycles.[74] But God revealed through Job hundreds of years before science learned the truth that the earth rotates in relation to the sun (Job 38:12–14).

Many Planets

The Bible reveals that the earth is not the only planet, but one among many (Hebrews 1:2).

The Oceans

Moses knew that the Atlantic Ocean, the Pacific Ocean, the Arctic Ocean, the Antarctic Ocean, the Indian Ocean, the Mediterranean Sea and the Asiatic Sea all lay in one bed, in one place. A ship can travel around the world without touching dirt because all the oceans are linked together. How did Moses know that when it took men hundreds of years to make that discovery? God told him (Genesis 1:9). Additionally it was not known until the 1970s that the oceans were fed with underground streams. It was thought the oceans were fed only by rain and rivers. But in Job 38:16, God told man thousands of years ago the scientific truth regarding their water supply.[75]

Man did not learn of gigantic mountains in the ocean until about a century ago. But Jonah declared over 2,000 years ago, "I sank beneath the waves, and the waters closed over me. Seaweed wrapped itself around my head. I sank down to the very roots of the mountains. I was imprisoned in the earth, whose gates lock shut forever. But you, O LORD my God, snatched me from the jaws of death" (Jonah 2:5-6 NLT).

Blood

The importance of blood in healing was not realized until several thousand years after Moses declared that "the life of the flesh is in the blood" (Leviticus 17:11). President George Washington likely would have survived his fatal illness had the doctor given him blood instead of draining it, which was a common practice known as bloodletting in that day. Medically it is known today that blood aids all the cells in the body and provides the food needed for healing.

Man's Body

Was Moses correct in saying that man was made from the dust of the earth over four thousand years ago (Genesis 2:7; 3:19)?

39

It is a scientific fact that the human body is comprised of some 28 base and trace elements, all of which can be found in the earth.[76] Christians believe that all mankind descends from the gene pool of the one man, Adam, as is taught in scripture (Genesis 5; Acts 17:26). However this truth for years was unknown. Researchers now know the Bible was correct. A 1995 study of a section of Y chromosomes from 38 men with different ethnicity from around the world was consistent with the Bible's teaching that all men came from the same man (Adam).[77]

Circumcision on the Eighth Day

Moses states that a newborn boy was to be circumcised on the eighth day (Genesis 17:12). Medical science has discovered that the eighth day for circumcision is ideal because the blood clotting chemical prothrombin peaks in a newborn at that time.[78] Obviously God told Moses this scientific fact.

The Noahic Flood

Though still refuted by many nonbelievers, fossil evidence verifies the Noahic flood that God sent as judgment upon the wicked. "When plants and animals die, they decompose rapidly. Yet billions of life forms around the globe have been preserved as fossils. Geologists now know that fossils only form if there is rapid deposition of life buried away from scavengers and bacteria. This agrees exactly with what the Bible says occurred during the global Flood."[79]

The Jet Stream

In a time when it was thought that the wind blew straight, Solomon declared, "The wind goeth toward the south, and turneth about unto the north; it whirleth about continually, and the wind returneth again according to his circuits." (Ecclesiastes 1:6). He wrote that 3,000 years ago, yet it wasn't until World War II that airmen discovered the jet stream circuit.[80]

ASK YOURSELF

What is the rationale for biblical revelation regarding scientific facts hundreds of years prior to their discovery by man?

How does such scientific information verify the Bible as divine in origin?

How might the documented evidence contained in this Hot Button supplement that of the previous two Hot Buttons in giving a defense for the Bible's authenticity?

In what ways did this Hot Button strengthen your belief in the Bible as God's Word?

Chapter 7   Is the Bible Reliable?
Personal Experience Answers

"And Jesus answered and said unto him, Blessed art thou, Simon Bar-jona: for flesh and blood hath not revealed it unto thee, but my Father which is in heaven."—Matthew 16: 17.

To the archeological, prophetic and scientific objective evidence for the Bible's being the Word of God, add the subjective evidence of personal experience. I know the Bible is the divine Word of God due to the Holy Spirit's illumination and confirmation to me that it is, and because it does what it says it will do for me, in me, and through me. Personally, I can point to promises and precepts in the Bible that have been fulfilled in my life regarding salvation, forgiveness, strength, comfort, service, and more, as can millions of other believers. A little boy had a tummyache, and his mother asked why? He said "I've been eating green apples."

The mother inquired, "How do you know it's the green apples that are causing the stomachache?"

"Because," the boy replied, "I have inside information."

How do I know the Bible is the Word of God? I have inside information. Every born-again believer does. "The Holy Spirit," declares R. A. Torrey, "sets His seal in the soul of every believer to the divine authority of the Bible. It is possible to get to a place where we need no argument to prove that the Bible is God's Word. Christ says, 'My sheep hear my voice.' God's children know His voice, and I know that the voice which speaks to me from the pages of that Book is the voice of my Father,....Everyone can have that testimony. John 7:17 tells you how to get it: 'If any man will do his will, he shall know of the doctrine, whether it be of God.'"[81]

John MacArthur states, "While the Christian can marshal good arguments from personal experience, science, archeology, and prophecy, he cannot 'prove' the Bible true and authoritative. Still, he knows the Bible is true because of his resident Truth Teacher—

the Holy Spirit. The Holy Spirit is the only One who can prove God's Word is true, and He does this as He works in the heart and mind of the Christian whom He indwells."[82]

Martin Luther said, "Man is like Lot's wife—a pillar of salt. He's like a log or a stone. He's like a lifeless statue that uses neither eyes nor mouth, neither senses nor heart, unless he is enlightened, converted and regenerated by the Holy Spirit."[83] The plain fact is that man needs spiritual illumination to see the Bible for what it really is, God's divinely inspired Book.

John Stott shares what I believe is the bottom line about the Bible in the believer's life. "The Christian is under both instruction and authority. He looks to Jesus as his Teacher to instruct him and as his Lord to command him. He believes what he believes because Jesus taught it, and he does what he does because Jesus told him to do it....Our view of Scripture is derived from Christ's view of Scripture, just as our view of discipleship, of Heaven and Hell, of the Christian life, and of everything else is derived from Jesus Christ. Any question about the inspiration of Scripture and its authority therefore resolves itself to: 'What did Jesus Christ teach about these points?'...To sum up, the authority of Scripture is due to the inspiration of Scripture. The Old and New Testaments are authoritative in our lives, because they are, in fact, inspired. And, therefore, since Jesus Christ is our Teacher as well as our Lord, the authority of Christ and the authority of Scripture stand or fall together."[84]

The Bible is God's Word. Therefore, as B. B. Warfield put it, "How unquestionably we must receive its statements of fact, bow before its enunciations of duty, tremble before its warnings, and rest upon its promises."[85] In studying the archeological, scientific, prophetic and experiential evidence for the authenticity of the Bible, one can only come to the same conclusion as that of Martin Luther. Luther stated, "Mighty potentates have raged against this Book and sought to destroy and uproot it—Alexander the Great and princes of Egypt and Babylon; the monarchs of Persia, of Greece, and of Rome; the Emperors Julius and Augustus—but they prevailed nothing. They are gone, while the Book remains; and it will remain forever and ever, perfect and entire as it was declared at first. Who has thus helped it—who has protected it against such mighty forces? No one, surely, but God Himself, who is Master of all things."[86]

ASK YOURSELF

How has the Holy Spirit confirmed the Bible as Truth to you personally?

Is it inconsistent for a believer to state that Christ is Lord (authority) in his or her life and yet have doubts about the Bible's authority?

What role does faith play in trusting the Bible?

How does Martin Luther's statement apply to the unspiritual man in regard to acceptance of the Bible? (1 Corinthians 2:14–16).

What, in essence, does John MacArthur state regarding "proof" of the Bible?

Summarize the four evidences for the divinity and authority of the Bible cited in Hot Buttons 4–7.

Chapter 8   The Existence of Evil

"Let no man say when he is tempted, I am tempted of God: for God cannot be tempted with evil, neither tempteth he any man."—James 1:13.

"This problem of evil is one to which we all must offer an answer, regardless of the belief system to which we subscribe."[87]—Ravi Zacharias

The present world of evil and suffering is not the world God created; it is the result of the fall of man into sin (man's selfishness and lust for more than what God designed—Genesis 3). God is love and the Author of love, not evil, and He desired to create man to love Him and to be loved by Him. But genuine love cannot exist apart from free will, the freedom for man to choose to love God or not. Adam and Eve in the garden chose to disobey God (choosing something that He had not designed or created), ushering evil into the world. Man's selfishness, choosing his way instead of God's way, precipitated evil. God is not evil nor the author of evil. Due to the fall (Genesis 3), the world is in an abnormal state (not as God designed). Man is separated from God until reconciled through Christ, nature at times works havoc on lives and land, man raises his ugly hand against man in violent acts, and even the animal world can be man's enemy. I emphasize again that none of these conditions existed in God's original creation prior to man's fall. [88]

This is the point John Calvin makes: "[T]he Lord had declared that everything that He had made…was exceedingly good (Gen. 1:31). Whence then comes this wickedness to man, that he should fall away from his God? Lest we should think it comes from creation, God had put His stamp of approval on what had come forth from Himself. By his own evil intention, then, man corrupted the pure nature he had received from the Lord and, by his fall, drew all his posterity with him into destruction. Accordingly, we should contemplate the evident cause of condemnation in the corrupt nature of humanity—which is closer to us—rather than seek a hidden and utterly incomprehensible cause in God's predestination."[89]

John MacArthur stated, "It is helpful, I think, to understand that sin is not itself a thing created. Sin is neither substance, being, spirit, nor matter. So it is technically not proper to think of sin as something that was created. Sin is simply a lack of moral perfection in a fallen creature. Fallen creatures themselves bear full responsibility for their sin. And all evil in the universe emanates from the sins of fallen creatures. For example, Romans 5:12 says that death entered the world because of sin. Death, pain, disease, stress, exhaustion, calamity, and all the bad things that happen came as a result of the entrance of sin into the universe (Genesis 3:14–24). All those evil effects of sin continue to work in the world and will be with us as long as sin is."[90]

"Have you ever wondered," asked Adrian Rogers, "why God doesn't obliterate the Devil and eradicate all sin? If God destroyed evil, God would destroy every opportunity of choice, for we would no longer have the freedom to choose good over evil. And if God were to destroy every opportunity for choice, then God would destroy every opportunity for us to choose freely to love. Therefore, God would destroy the highest good. For God to destroy evil would be evil. God doesn't destroy evil; instead, God defeats evil. How? Through Calvary and the resurrection, God turns every hurt into a hallelujah; every defeat into victory!"[91]

The good news is that paradise lost will one day be regained. Evil, though present, is only temporary. Upon Christ's return to earth, evil will be eternally banished—no more tears, sorrow, suffering, sickness or death, and "the wolf and the lamb shall feed together" (Isaiah 65:25). What a glorious day that will be!

The Existence of Evil

ASK YOURSELF

In God's original creation, was evil present?

What is the source of evil in the world?

How does the fall impact all of nature and mankind?

Why does God permit evil in the world, according to Adrian Rogers?

Is sin something that God created?

Who is to blame for the suffering, sickness, and pain in the world?

When will evil be forever conquered and banished, resulting in the regaining of the paradise that was lost?

Chapter 9   Creationism vs. Evolution

"He created all things in heaven and on earth, visible and invisible. Whether they are kings or lords, rulers or powers—everything has been created through him and for him." —Colossians 1:16, GWT.

God states that He created the heavens and the earth. This is in direct contrast to evolutionists who insist the world originated from a big bang. It is not just conservative ministers who reject evolution. Numbered among the opponents to evolution and supporters of creation are many of the greatest, brightest scientists who've ever lived, including Michael Faraday, Lord Kelvin, Joseph Lister, Louis Pasteur, Isaac Newton, Johannes Kepler, Sir William Ramsey, and Lord Francis Bacon.[92]

Hear the testimonials of some of the world's sharpest minds regarding evolution.

"Scientists who go about teaching that evolution is a fact of life are great con men, and the story they are telling may be the greatest hoax ever. In explaining evolution, we do not have one iota of fact."[93] —Dr. Newton Tahmisian, a physiologist for the Atomic Energy Commission

"The evolutional theory is purely the product of the imagination."[94] —Sir Ambrose Fleming, president of the Philosophical Society of Great Britain

"I believe that, one day, the Darwinian myth will be ranked the greatest deceit in the history of science. When this happens, many people will pose the question, 'How did this ever happen?'"[95] —Swedish embryologist, Dr. Søren Løvtrup

"Evolution is a theory universally accepted—not because it can be proved by logically coherent evidence to be true, but because the only alternative, special creation, is clearly incredible."[96] —Scientist D. M. S. Watson

"There is no evidence which would show man developing step-by-step from lower forms of life. There is nothing to show that man was in any way connected with monkeys. He appeared suddenly and in substantially the same form as he is today. There are no such things as missing links. So far as concerns the major groups of animals, the creationists appear to have the best argument. There is not the slightest evidence that any one of the major groups arose from any other."[97]—Biologist at Smithsonian

Evolution Is a Religion, Not a Science

Wikipedia encyclopedia defines science (from the Latin *scientia,* meaning "knowledge") "as an enterprise that builds and organizes knowledge in the form of testable explanations and predictions about the world. An older and closely related meaning still in use today is that of Aristotle, for whom scientific knowledge was a body of reliable knowledge that can be logically and rationally explained."[98] Evolution doesn't meet the criteria to be classified as a science. It cannot be tested, studied, observed and certainly not rationally explained!

Dr. Henry Morris, Institute for Creation Research, stated "Evolutionists often insist that evolution is a proved fact of science, providing the very framework of scientific interpretation, especially in the biological sciences. This, of course, is nothing but wishful thinking. Evolution is not even a scientific hypothesis, since there is no conceivable way in which it can be tested. As a matter of fact, many leading evolutionists have recognized the essentially 'religious' character of evolutionism."[99]

"The notion that natural evolutionary processes," states John MacArthur, "can account for the origin of all living species has never been and never will be established as fact. Nor is it 'scientific' in any true sense of the word. Science deals with what can be observed and reproduced by experimentation. The origin of life can be neither observed nor reproduced in any laboratory. By definition, then, true science can give us no knowledge whatsoever about where we came from or how we got here. Belief in evolutionary theory is a matter of sheer faith. And dogmatic belief in any naturalistic theory is no more 'scientific' than any other kind of religious faith."[100]

Foundation of Evolution

Josh McDowell states that the case for evolution rests on the assumption that three events have happened. However, McDowell says, none have been observed in action.

Evolution Assumes That Order Can Emerge Naturally Out of Chaos

"No law of nature," states McDowell, "can account for order coming out of chaos. The idea contradicts inviolable laws of entropy, which say, in a nutshell, that life always plays out into death; the organic decays into the inorganic. Stars burn out and disintegrate. Planets slow infinitesimally with each orbit. Energy is consumed, and we consistently observe a universe that is irrevocably running down.

Evolution Assumes That All Life Emerged from Dead Matter

Never in the history of our world has anyone caused life to start up from dead matter or witnessed such a phenomenon. No one has ever been able to create a single organic cell or bring a dead cell to life even under the most carefully controlled laboratory conditions.

Evolution Assumes That Human Intelligence and Reason Evolved from Dead Matter

According to the theory, no thinking, reasoning organisms existed when the big bang went off. What principle operating in nature accounts for the spontaneous appearance of a self-aware, thinking organism arising out of formless gases and inanimate minerals? The answer is simple: There is no such force or principle. Nothing can give more than it has. A universe that begins in lifeless chaos will remain lifeless and chaotic. Yet evolution asks us to suspend reason and assume an exception has occurred, despite the fact that no exception has ever been observed or demonstrated."[101]

The best and only reasonable explanation for the existence of the universe and all within it is that an intelligent designer created it. The Bible, God's authoritative Word, repetitively declares that the world and all within it was made by God (Genesis 1:1).

Questions to Ask Evolutionists

"The test of any theory," according to Dr. Kent Hovind, "is whether or not it provides answers to basic questions. Some well-meaning but misguided people think evolution is a reasonable theory to explain man's questions about the universe. Evolution is not a good theory—it is just a pagan religion masquerading as science."[102] Hovind suggests the following questions for the evolutionist.[103] How did matter get so perfectly organized? Where did the energy come from to do all the organizing? When, where, why, and how did life come from dead matter? When, where, why, and how did: a) single-celled plants become multicelled (Where are the two- and three-celled intermediates?); b) single-celled animals evolve; c) fish change to amphibians; d) amphibians change to reptiles; e) reptiles change to birds (The lungs, bones, eyes, reproductive organs, heart, method of locomotion, body covering, etc., are all very different!)? How did the intermediate forms live?

Which evolved first—how, and how long, did it work without the others—a) the digestive system, the food to be digested, the appetite, the ability to find and eat the food, the digestive juices, or the body's resistance to its own digestive juices (stomach, intestines, etc.); b) the drive to reproduce or the ability to reproduce; c) the lungs, the mucus lining to protect them, the throat, or the perfect mixture of gases to be breathed into the lungs; d) DNA or RNA to carry the DNA message to cell parts; e) the termite or the flagella in its intestines that actually digest the cellulose; f) the plants or the insects that live on and pollinate the plants; g) the bones, ligaments, tendons, blood supply, or muscles to move the bones; h) the nervous system, repair system, or hormone system; i) the immune system or the need for it?

The Pivotal Question to Ask Evolutionists

Ken Ham, founder of *Answers in Genesis,* suggests an additional question to ask those who oppose creationism. "What caused the universe to come into existence, and where did the original energy or matter come from?" Ham states that this is a foundational question to ask evolutionists, for without a cause (and a mass/energy source), there can be no big bang, evolution of stars, or life.[104]

The evidence leading us to prefer the idea that God created all that exists over the theory of evolution is additionally mirrored by the very reasons for God's existence as cited in Hot Button #2.

Paul Ackerman, in his book *It's a Young World After All,* says this. "Let me be blunt on this matter. Evolutionists around the world have had to learn the hard way that evolution cannot stand up against creationism in any fair and impartial debate situation where the stakes are the hearts and minds of intelligent, undecided but nevertheless objective and open-minded audiences. Experience will prove that the same is true for the age issue as well. Evolutionists' beliefs regarding the origin and development of life cannot withstand the scrutiny of an informed opposition, and neither can evolutionists' claim to the effect that the universe has existed for ten to twenty billion years, and the earth for 4.5 billion years. To delay the collapse of widespread public acceptance of such claims, it will be necessary for evolutionist scientists to carefully avoid debate."[105] And so they do.

ASK YOURSELF

What to you is the greatest evidence for creation?

Why is evolution a religion and not a science?

According to Ken Ham, what is the pivotal question to ask evolutionists?

To what degree is the view of evolution prevalent in the classroom at your school?

If you were asked to substantiate creationism over evolution, what might you state?

Additional support for creationism may be found in contacting the Institute for Creation Research (ICR.org) and Answers in Genesis (AnswersinGenesis.org).

Chapter 10   Are All Religions the Same, Deep Down?

"For Satan himself transforms himself into an angel of light."—2 Corinthians 11:14 Darby.

Sixty-three percent of churchgoing, supposedly Christian teens, according to Frank Barna, believe that "Muslims, Buddhists, Christians, Jews and all other people pray to the same God, even though they use different names for their god."[106] Sixty-five percent either believe or suspect that there is "no way to tell which religion is true."[107] Their view of God is so flawed that they are not certain that Jesus Christ is man's only means of salvation or getting to Heaven.

In a witnessing encounter I had, a religious man told me that religion was like traveling to a destination; there are many roads that lead to the same place, and it didn't matter which one was taken. Is he right? Does it matter what a person believes, as long as he or she is serious in that belief? Are all religions basically the same deep down? Will those who travel various "religious" roads that differ from the tenets of Christianity end up in Heaven? The Bible holds the answer.

To state that all religions are the same is just factually untrue. "No one ever makes this claim," says Peter Kreeft, "unless he is 1) abysmally [terribly] ignorant of what the different religions of the world actually teach, or 2) intellectually irresponsible in understanding these teachings in the vaguest and woolliest way, or 3) morally irresponsible in being indifferent to them."[108] In regard to religion, what looks the same is not necessarily the same. Two white pills look the same in every detail, but the purpose of one is to heal (aspirin), and the purpose of the other is to kill (arsenic). Two apples look the same, but one is artificial (fake), and the other is the real thing (genuine). Religions may appear to be same, but they are not. To know the Truth, one must dig beyond the surface.

57

In what ways is Christianity different from the world religions?

It Is Unique in Its Founder

Jesus Christ claimed to be God in the flesh (John 8:58; 10:30) and validated the claim in rising from the dead (Matthew 28:5–7). No other religious founder who ever made such a claim succeeded in backing it up. Jesus' tomb alone bears the "Vacancy" sign of the dead. Jesus is unique in the sinless life He lived. Muslims will admit that Muhammad was sinful, and Buddhists do not claim perfection for Siddhartha Gautama Buddha. Christianity stands or falls upon its Founder, but not so with religions. Remove Muhammad from Islam, and Islam remains. *He* is not critical to Islam; just what he communicated about Allah and his will is critically important to this religion. Remove Buddha from Buddhism, and Buddhism remains. Buddhism rests basically on the teachings of Buddha, not Buddha himself, who is not essential to the quest for a tranquil life through a disciplined mind. Remove Confucius from Confucianism, and Confucianism remains. Its founder, Confucius, is inconsequential. But remove Christ from Christianity, and it will crumble. Christ's identity is essential. Christianity is based upon His death, burial and resurrection and claim to be the eternal Son of God, not just on His ethical and moral teachings.[109]

Christianity Is Unique in Its Means of Salvation

Christianity is also the only religion (faith) that recognizes the hopeless gap between man and a Holy God, embracing the view that salvation can only be obtained through God's grace (Ephesians 2:8–9). All other religions include a works agenda in their means of acquiring heaven or whatever destination they aspire to. Two letters in the word *done* define the uniqueness of Christianity with regard to salvation. All other religions say to be saved you have to *do* something; Christianity says to be saved you must trust in what Christ already has *done.*

Christianity's Holy Book, the Bible, Is Unique

There is no other book like the Bible. Christians believe the Bible is God's only written revelation to man. It took 40 different men more than 1,500 years to write the Bible's 66 books. Its storyline is unified with no contradictions. "More than 5,000 manuscripts of the New Testament exist today, which makes the New Testament the best-attested document of all ancient writings."[110] Hundreds of biblical prophecies have been fulfilled, giving added attestation to its divine authorship.

Christianity is a faith-based relationship with Jesus Christ, not a religion, and it is incompatible with world religions. Religion is man's reaching up to God; Christianity is God's reaching down to man. John MacArthur stated, "If we believe the Bible, we cannot concede that other religions might be true as well. If we believe that Christ is Lord of all, and if we truly love Him, we cannot countenance the doctrines of those who deny Him (1 Corinthians 16:22). Christianity, if true at all, is exclusively true. Inherent in the claims of Christ is the assertion that He alone offers truth, and all religious systems that deviate from His truth are false. Jesus said, 'I am the way, the truth, and the life: no man cometh unto the Father, but by me' (John 14:6). If this is true, every other religion is a lie" (Romans 3:4).[111]

ASK YOURSELF

Are all religions the same? Why or why not?

How does the founder of Christianity differ from the founders of other religions?

In what ways is Jesus unique?

Outside of Christ, in what other ways is Christianity unique?

Does a personal faith-based relationship with God distinguish Christianity from world religions?

Does it matter what "religion" one embraces, and, if so, why?

What supports MacArthur's contention that Christianity is the only true religion [faith]?

Chapter 11 Will a Loving God Send a Person to Hell?

"And whosoever was not found written in the book of life was cast into the lake of fire."—Revelation 20:15.

"The vague and tenuous hope that God is too kind to punish the ungodly has become a deadly opiate for the consciences of millions."[112]—A. W. Tozer

At the time of this writing, grave controversy is erupting regarding Bob Bell's book, *Love Wins: A Book About Heaven, Hell, and the Fate of Every Person Who Has Ever Lived.* Bell, in essence, advocates that God is not angry about anything and therefore will not punish anybody for all eternity in a literal Hell.[113] Undoubtedly missing in Bell's Bible are Psalm 7:11, which declares, "God judgeth the righteous, and God is angry with the wicked every day"; and Revelation 20:15: "And whosoever was not found written in the book of life was cast into the lake of fire." Students need to be armed with sound doctrine to withstand the heretical attacks of false teachers such as Bell.

Jesus' story (not parable) of the rich man and Lazarus reveals the sordid nature of Hell (Luke 16:19–31) and reflects the six "P" words which we can use to describe this literal abode of eternal punishment.

A Place of Pain

Unimaginable physical and mental torment will be experienced in Hell. There will be varying degrees of punishment in Hell (Matthew 10:15; 11:22, 24; Mark 6:11; Hebrews 10:29). "In one form or another the word 'torment' occurs [sixteen] times in the New Testament....In the case of Hell's torments, this suffering will last forever. Over 1,500 years ago, the great preacher John Chrysostom emphasized what this will mean. "The damned shall suffer an end without end, a death without death, a decay without decay....They shall have punishment without pity, misery without mercy, sorrow without succor, crying without comfort, torment without ease."[114]

A Place of Passion

Insatiable appetites and desires plague the inhabitants of Hell.

A Place of Parting

The unsaved are separated forever from the redeemed.

A Place of Prayer

The eternally damned will come to see their need of God, but too late. People in Hell will weep, wail, and gnash their teeth, crying out to God for salvation—but in vain.

A Place of Permeating Darkness

Jude describes Hell as "the blackness of darkness for ever" (Jude 13). Utter blackness makes relationships impossible in Hell. C. S. Lewis declares Hell as a place of "nothing but yourself for all eternity"! The inhabitants of Hell know only isolation and loneliness. There are no friendships or fellowship.

A Place of Permanence

Hell has no exits. There is no way out, so there is no hope for its inhabitants. Yet, the worst aspect of Hell is that God is not there!

This awful place called Hell was originally created for Satan and the demons, not man. "Then He will also say to those on His left, 'Depart from Me, accursed ones, into the eternal fire which has been prepared for the devil and his angels'" (Matthew 25:41 NASB). Adrian Rogers comments, "If you go to Hell, you'll be an intruder. Hell was not prepared for you. It was prepared for the Devil and his angels. But if you choose to follow Satan, you'll follow him to Hell."[115] The plain fact is that God does not want any person to go to

Hell. Peter bears this truth out in stating, "The Lord is not slack concerning his promise, as some men count slackness; but is longsuffering to us-ward, not willing that any should perish, but that all should come to repentance" (2 Peter 3:9). God has placed in the path of every person en route to Hell the biggest roadblock possible, the Cross of Christ. If a man dies and goes to Hell, it will be because of ignoring the Cross. In truth, God doesn't send anyone to Hell; man goes there by choice. "And ye will not come to me, that ye might have life" (John 5:40). G. K. Chesterton once remarked, "Hell is God's great compliment to the reality of human freedom and the dignity of human personality." Hell, a compliment? Yes, because God is saying to us, "You are significant. I take you seriously. Choose to reject Me; choose Hell if you will. I will let you go."[116]

C. S. Lewis summarizes the issue well in stating, "The door of Hell is locked on the inside. All those who go to Hell will to be there and to stay there....There are only two kinds of people in the end: those who say to God, 'Thy will be done,' and those to whom God says, in the end, 'Thy will be done.' All that are in Hell choose it."[117]

Why doesn't God force everyone to love Him so no one goes to Hell? God created man as free moral beings. To compel or force man to love Him would violate that freedom. To force man to spend eternity in Heaven with a God they reject would be unfair; thus, a place of separation from God forever is afforded.

J. I. Packer states that many protestant theologians and cultists have adopted an "annihilationism or conditionalism" view of Hell.[118] John Ankerberg, in support of Packer, proposes seven excellent reasons to reject such views that deny an eternal Hell. These are: "1) Jesus Christ is the principle figure responsible for the doctrine of eternal punishment. The denial of eternal punishment is tantamount to the denial of the deity of our Lord and Savior. 2) Rejection of Hell is a denial of biblical authority which opens the door to additional revisionist and syncretistic tendencies in other areas. To reject scriptural truth at one point is to be able to reject scriptural truth at any point and thereby to substitute human speculation for divine revelation. 3) The problem is not a scriptural issue, but an emotional issue, contaminated by secularist and humanistic thinking. 4) To reject eternal punishment and accept other ways of salvation is to affirm that the cross of Christ was unnecessary. 5) To affirm universalism is the denial of the church's mission to preach the Gospel and warn men to escape God's wrath and eternal punishment (2 Corinthians 5:11; Luke 3:7, 9, 17, 18). 6) The doctrine of eternal punishment is the watershed between evangelical and nonevangelical thought. 7) Universalism logically repudiates the doctrine of justification by faith."[119]

Commenting on whose names are in the Lamb's Book of Life, Paige Patterson surmises, "In Chapter 20 of the Revelation, a search has been made in the Lamb's Book of Life. Those whose names are not included, regardless of status in the present age, are cast into the lake of fire. Unfortunately, the only conclusion conceivable is that those who are blood-bought sinners whose names are entered in the Book of Life are saved, while all others are forever excluded. This was not God's design for man. The everlasting fires of Hell were prepared for the Devil and his angels (Matthew 25:41), but God is so gracious that He never coerces anyone to make Him the object of his affection and adore Him. If there is rejection of His overtures, then the only option is the place called Hell."[120]

Imagine being hopelessly lost in the deep forest at midnight when a light appears. Acting upon the light, you discover its source—the burning headlamps of a jeep. Upon the hood of the jeep is a detailed map showing the way out of the forest. Immediately you tear the map into small pieces and demolish the headlamps of the jeep. Sounds absurd, does it not? In this scenario, what person would be responsible for your remaining lost? Certainly not the one who provided the jeep, headlamps, or map! Sadly, this is often man's response to the light God provides through missionaries, evangelists, pastors, and the Bible. By rejection of the gospel light, man chooses his own destiny in Hell.

On one occasion when Vice President Calvin Coolidge was presiding over a Senate meeting, one senator angrily told another to go "straight to Hell." The offended senator complained to Coolidge. Coolidge, having leafed through the rule book while listening to the heated debate, responded, "I've looked through the rule book. You don't have to go."[121] Neither you nor anyone else has to go to Hell. God has made a way of escape.

ASK YOURSELF

How do you reconcile God's love and eternal judgment?

Whom does God send to Hell?

Summarize C. S. Lewis' statement about "the door" to Hell?

Why doesn't God force man to love Him so Hell may be avoided?

What are the seven reasons, according to John Ankerberg, for the affirmation of Hell?

What has God done to make Hell escapable (prior to going there)?

For whom was Hell originally designed?

Explain Adrian Rogers' statement that all who go to Hell go as intruders.

Watch a one-minute presentation on "How Can a Loving God Send People To Hell?" by Lee Strobel on YouTube (type this heading into the search link).

Chapter 12 Questions and Answers about Heaven

"Thou shalt guide me with thy counsel, and afterward receive me to glory."—Psalm 73:24.

Hopefully this *Hot Button,* as it increases knowledge of the reality and nature of Heaven, will comfort those who are broken-hearted due to the death of a saved loved one by granting sure hope of seeing him or her again, motivate the believer to greater devotion and service to Christ, inflame the heart of the non-Christian with a desire to make preparation to go there, impassion the saint to evangelize others in Christ's name so they may also go to Heaven, and incite excitement about what awaits the redeemed at the end of this life. Whereas Scripture answers many questions about Heaven, it remains silent about many others.

Is Heaven a Place?

Jesus states that it is a place (John 14:2). It is a place just as much as the city in which you reside is a place. If it were not, the Bible would not speak of its streets of pure gold, walls of jasper, foundations of twelve precious stones and gates of pearl, or its inhabitants. To the liberals who claim this description of Heaven is simply figurative language, Jesus responds, "If it were not so, I would have told you." In other words, Jesus is saying, "If Heaven were not like I described it, I would have told you so!" Believers must remember that besides the little we know about Heaven, there is far more that we do not know. Paul affirms this truth: "But as it is written, Eye hath not seen, nor ear heard, neither have entered into the heart of man, the things which God hath prepared for them that love him" (1 Corinthians 2:9). The best description of Heaven fails to touch the hem of its awesome glorious garment.

"To those who doubt the existence of Heaven because, no matter how far we travel in space, we have yet to locate it, consider the following facts. The distance between the electrons and the nucleus of an atom being proportionate to the distance between

Pluto and the sun, all matter on this earth is comprised of ninety-five percent space—leaving plenty of room for an unseen dimension to coexist with the material world we presently perceive."[122]

Will Heaven Be a Blast or a Bore?

"Heaven will not be the boring experience of strumming a harp on a cloud, as some facetiously characterize it," stated Paul Little. "It will be the most dynamic, expanding, exhilarating experience conceivable. Our problem now is that, with our finite minds, we cannot imagine it."[123] The theologian Jon Courson makes an excellent observation. "When Jesus says, 'I go to prepare a place for you,' He is not speaking generically, but specifically. Jesus is preparing a place for you specifically. Think through this. What do you enjoy? What has God built into your being? Whatever it is, know this. Jesus is preparing a place for you to fulfill the elements He's woven into the fabric of your personality uniquely and specifically."[124]

Will We Know One Another in Heaven?

"For now we see through a glass, darkly; but then face to face: now I know in part; but then shall I know even as also I am known" (1 Corinthians 13:12). In their heavenly (resurrected) bodies, Jesus, Moses, and Elijah were recognized (John 20:16; Matthew 17:1–4). Jesus said that we will see "Abraham, and Isaac, and Jacob, and all the prophets, in the kingdom of God" (Luke 13:28). I believe part of the comfort Paul refers to for believers in 1 Thessalonians 4:14–18 is knowledge of a reunion day coming in Heaven with loved ones. The saints in Heaven will fellowship not only with their redeemed marriage mates, parents, children, grandparents, and friends, but also with all other redeemed people not known to the believer during life on earth. This includes the prophets, disciples, patriarchs, missionaries, and evangelists.

David prayed and fasted for his baby seven days and nights, but the baby died (2 Samuel 12:18–23). The servants were fearful of telling David the news of the baby's death; they imagined it would completely devastate him. David noticed them whispering to each other and inquired, "Is the child dead?" In learning of the child's death, David reacted in the opposite manner to that which the servants expected. Instead of "losing it," he bathed, changed clothing, went to worship God, and then asked for food to eat. The servants asked David why he had reacted this way. He replied, "I fasted and wept while the child was alive, for I said, 'Perhaps the Lord will be gracious to me and let the child live.' But why should I fast when he is dead? Can I bring him back again? I will go to him one day, but he cannot return to me" (2 Samuel 12:22–23 NLT). This narrative teaches that your child on earth will be your child in Heaven; and, thus, your mother will be your mother, your father be your father, and so on. Obviously the role in the relationship will change in Heaven, but the relationship will continue. W. A. Criswell, in *Heaven,* states that one's personality survives in Heaven, that we each will be who we are now but without the baggage of sin and imperfection.[125] Further, Criswell states, "We shall not know less of each other in Heaven; we shall know more. We shall possess our individual names in Heaven. We shall be known as individuals. You will be you; I shall be I; we shall be we. Personality and individuality exist beyond the grave."[126]

Who Is Granted Access to Heaven?

Heaven is the eternal dwelling place of the redeemed family of God. The *entrance ticket* into this celestial city is not church membership, baptism, confirmation, righteousness, or good deeds, but a personal relationship with Jesus Christ through the new birth (John 3:3; Acts 20:21). Jesus, in discussing His ascension to Heaven to make preparation for the saints, was asked by Thomas to clarify the way to this celestial abode (John 14:5). Jesus answered Thomas, "I am the way, the truth, and the life: no man cometh unto the Father, but by me" (John 14:6). Jesus is the only *Door* to this celestial city (John 10:9).

What Will Be the Spiritual Condition of Those in Heaven?

"We shall be unblamable and unreprovable," proclaimed C. H. Spurgeon, "even in His eyes. His law will not only have no charge against us, but it will be magnified in us. Moreover, the work of the Holy Spirit within us will be altogether complete. He will make us so perfectly holy that we shall have no lingering tendency to sin. Judgment, memory, will—every power and passion shall be emancipated from the thraldom [captivity] of evil. We shall be holy even as God is holy, and in His presence we shall dwell forever. Saints will not be out of place in Heaven; their beauty will be as great as that of the place prepared for them."[127]

What Kinds of Living Quarters Are in Heaven?

In Heaven there are "many mansions" (John 14:2). Heaven was designed to accommodate the innumerable multitudes who would enter its domain. There is no danger of insufficient housing for the ransomed of God. Jesus' use of the term "mansions" (rooms or apartments) indicates distinct, private accommodations for each of His children.[128] The believer's apartment in Heaven will never need maintenance or replacement, for it is eternally durable.

Will Some Saints Receive Positions in Heaven Greater Than That of Others?

Revelation 21:14 speaks of the twelve foundations of the wall of Heaven bearing the names of the twelve apostles. Obviously the twelve apostles will therefore occupy positions of greater preeminence in Heaven than others. Abraham had a position in Heaven of greater prominence and authority than that of Lazarus (Luke 16:22–31). James and John requested a seat at Jesus' right and left hands in Glory (Mark 10:37). To this request Jesus responded, "But to sit on my right hand and on my left hand is not mine to give; but it shall be given to them *for whom it is prepared*" (Mark 10:40, italics added). Jonathan Edwards, in preaching upon this subject, said, "Some are designed to sit in higher places there than others; some are designed to be advanced to higher degrees of honor and glory than others are....Though they are all seats of exceeding honor and blessedness, yet some are more so than others."[129] Jesus' parable of the pounds teaches this truth (Luke 19:11–27).

What Will Our Bodies Be Like in Heaven?

Jesus' resurrection body is the prototype for the redeemed of God (1 Cor. 15:20, 48–49; Phil. 3:21; 1 John 3:2). In the resurrection body, He walked, talked and ate (John 21:1–14). Jesus even dismissed the idea that saints in the afterlife would be "disembodied spirits" (Luke 24:37–39). The saint's spirit immediately at death enters the presence of the Lord; later, at the rapture of the church, it will be reunited with its body, which will be transformed into a glorified body likened to that of Christ (1 Thessalonians 4:16; 1 John 3:2).

Will We Know If Family Members or Friends Don't Arrive in Heaven?

The Bible indicates that unsaved family members or friends will not be remembered in Heaven. "Let his posterity be cut off; and in the generation following let their name be blotted out" (Psalm 109:13). "Thou shalt blot out the remembrance of Amalek from under heaven" (Deuteronomy 25:19). "Let them be blotted out of the book of the living, and not be written with the righteous" (Psalm 69:28). "Thou hast rebuked the heathen, thou hast destroyed the wicked, thou hast put out their name for ever and ever" (Psalm 9:5).

What Will We Do in Heaven?

Saints will serve God day and night (Revelation 7:15). Christians who do not delight in that now are in for a big change in Heaven. "There'll be no idleness in Heaven. We will serve Him with perfect joy and happiness."[130] This service implies judging and ruling the world and the angels with God (Luke 19:17–19; 1 Corinthians 6:2–3).

71

Saints will sing in Heaven (Revelation 5:9). The song of the redeemed in Heaven is "Worthy is the Lamb that was slain to receive power, and riches, and wisdom, and strength, and honour, and glory, and blessing" (Revelation 5:12). Worship of God is never ceasing.

Saints will rest in Heaven (Revelation 14:13). It has been said a person enters this world crying and goes out sighing. The saint gets tired and worn with the demands of livelihood and battling the foes of darkness, but 'a day of rest' (Hebrews 4:9) is coming for the redeemed when he 'will lay his sword down by the riverside and study war no more.' A Christian works, knowing the labor will end with eternal rest in the Father's presence.

Saints will socialize in Heaven. "Jesus speaks of the shrewd servant's desire to use earthly resources so that 'people will welcome me into their houses.' Then Jesus tells his followers to use 'worldly wealth' (earthly resources) to 'gain friends' (by making a difference in their lives on earth), 'so that when it is gone [when life on earth is over], you will be welcomed into eternal dwellings' (Luke 16:9). Our 'friends' in Heaven appear to be those whom we've touched in a significant way on earth. They will apparently have their own 'eternal dwellings.' Luke 16:9 suggests these eternal dwelling places of friends could be places to fellowship and stay in as we move about the heavenly kingdom."[131]

W. A. Criswell stated, "We shall not be passive spectators, just observing; but we shall be an active, vital part of the whole re-created kingdom of God. We each shall have a service to render according to how God has made us and endowed us. As we differ in tastes, likes, looks, choices, and abilities, so also we shall differ in our separate assignments and activities."[132]

Is There Cause for Sorrow in Heaven?

Heaven is "Hallelujah Square," because everybody is healthy and happy, freed from the grip of pain, sickness, crippling illness, suffering, and the constant pull of Satan toward sin (Revelation 21:4). The unpleasant and painful things of this life are vanquished from this holy city (Revelation 22:3).

What Are the Rewards Believers May Obtain in Heaven?

The Bible states at least five rewards the believer may receive.

• The Crown of Life—for the persecuted saint who endures suffering for the cause of Christ (Revelation 2:10);

• The Crown of Rejoicing—for the soul winner (1 Thessalonians 2:19; Philippians 4:1);

• The Crown of Righteousness—for believers who look for Jesus' return (2 Timothy 4:8);

• The Crown of Glory—for pastors who faithfully proclaim Christ and Him crucified, feed the flock of God, exhibit spiritual oversight for the flock of God, and lead by worthy example (1 Peter 5:1–4);

• The Incorruptible Crown—for the believer who, like an athlete, disciplines the body into subjection to Christ and becomes victorious over the flesh and who faithfully runs the Christian race to the finish line (1 Corinthians 9:24–27).

At What Moment Do We Enter Heaven?

Paul pointedly states that to be absent from the body is to be present with the Lord (2 Corinthians 5:8). At the moment that Lazarus died, angels escorted him into the presence of God in Heaven (Luke 16:22). The saint shuts his eyes in death and opens them instantly in Heaven. The epitaph on the tombstone of Solomon Peas, London, England, expresses this biblical truth.

Beneath these clouds and beneath these trees
Lies the body of Solomon Peas.
This is not Peas; it is only his pod.
Peas has shelled out and gone Home to God.[133]

How Do We Get to Heaven?

At least one man is known to have been escorted to Heaven by angels upon his death (Luke 16:22). Jesus assures the saints that He personally will escort them into Heaven at His coming (John 14:3). One fact is most certain. God will make sure His children arrive safely in Heaven. In light of this truth, there is no reason to fear nor for your heart to be troubled (John 14:1) that you will be sent to Hell accidentally.

Do Saints in Heaven Know What's Happening on Earth?

It is believed by some theologians that the cloud of witnessses encircling the believer referred to in Hebrews 12:1 are the redeemed in Heaven. Though I draw comfort from that thought, a closer inspection of the context does not yield that conclusion. The "Wherefore" of Hebrews 12:1 points back to the martyrs of the faith honored in the previous chapter, saints who endured grave suffering and death for the cause of the Gospel. Kenneth Wuest states, "The word [witnesses] does not include in its meaning the idea of a person looking at something. Peter uses it of himself (1 Pet. 5:1) as a witness of the sufferings of Christ; that is, one who has been retained and commissioned to testify to the sufferings of Christ which he has seen."[134] In summary, the "cloud of witnesses" of Hebrews 12:1 are the heroes of the faith who endured hardship, suffering, and death for the cause of Christ, who now are cheering us [not in being a spectator of our lives, but a lofty example of the life that overcomes] to "press on, fear not, and complete the race."

Saints in Heaven rejoice over souls that are saved on earth. Whether they are told of the news or they see it happen is unknown (Luke 15:7). From Heaven, Abraham and Lazarus saw the rich man in Hell (Luke 16:23–26). It is plausible to think that if a person in Heaven could see what was happening in Hell, then he likewise could see what was happening on earth at least to some degree, but this is mere conjecture. Additionally, in the same narrative, the rich man in Hell knows that all five of his brothers are still unsaved (Luke 16:27–28). Samuel's knowledge in Heaven of what was occurring on earth between King Saul and Israel (1 Samuel 28:16–18) supports the view that saints in Heaven will be informed of what transpires on earth, at least to some extent, as does the request of the martyrs in Heaven to know how much longer it would be before their persecutors would be punished (Revelation 6:9–10).

The only truth that may be categorically stated is that saints in Heaven have access to knowledge to some degree of world happenings. All else is mere speculation.

Will Children Who Die in Infancy or Prior to the Age of Understanding Enter Heaven?

David said regarding the death of his infant child, "I will go to him one day, but he cannot return to me" (2 Samuel 12:23). David was certain he would see his son in the eternal abode called Heaven. God included this story in Scripture, knowing that David would not be the only parent who would grieve the loss of a dearly loved child, so as to grant comfort and assurance of seeing him or her again. Man becomes accountable for sin when ability develops to comprehend its presence, its power, its penalty, and the provision of forgiveness (atonement and justification through the cross of Christ). The Christian parent can be confident of a grand reunion day with children who die before having attained this state or level of understanding.

How Much Knowledge Will We Possess in Heaven?

John MacArthur answers, "In Heaven we will also have perfect knowledge. Paul writes, 'Then I shall know just as I also am known' (1 Cor. 13:12). We will have no more unanswered questions, no confusion, no ignorance, and no more need to walk by faith rather than by sight."[135]

"Remember that you will one day be like Him," states C. H. Spurgeon, "when you see Him as He is; you shall not be so great as He is, you shall not be so divine, but still you shall, in measure, share the same honors and enjoy the same happiness and the same dignity which He possesses."[136]

Why So Little Talk and Excitement among Believers about Heaven?

"If there be so certain and glorious a rest for the saints," writes Richard Baxter, "why is there no more industrious seeking after it? One would think, if a man did but once hear of such unspeakable glory to be obtained, and believed what he heard to be true, he should be transported with the vehemency of his desire after it and should almost forget to eat and drink and should care for nothing else and speak of and inquire after nothing else but how to get this treasure. And yet people who hear of it daily and profess to believe it as a fundamental article of their faith do as little mind it or labor for it as if they had never heard of any such thing or did not believe one word they hear."[137] Knowledge of a personal reservation in Heaven made by Jesus Christ ought to put believers on shouting ground and liberate their lips to speak much of what awaits the saved at the end of this life.

> Sing the wondrous love of Jesus;
> Sing His mercy and His grace.
> In the mansions bright and blessed,
> He'll prepare for us a place.
> When we all get to Heaven,
> What a day of rejoicing that will be!
> When we all see Jesus,
> We'll sing and shout the victory![138]

ASK YOURSELF

What is the most fascinating thing about Heaven to you, and why?

Does the fact that rewards will be given in Heaven to saints who meet certain criteria motivate greater faithfulness and devotion to God?

How important is it to you that in Heaven loved ones will be known?

Why is Heaven a blast and not a bore?

What is the "ticket" that grants a person entrance into this celestial city, and do you possess it?

What leads you to think that many Christians are not too excited about Heaven? Why?

Knowing that Heaven or Hell awaits all people at the end of life, how should this fact influence your soul-winning efforts?

What are the bases for believing in the reality of Heaven?

Chapter 13   Predestined to Hell? No!

"He died in our place to take away our sins, and not only our sins but the sins of all people."– 1 John 2:2 NCV

"Who are the elect? The elect are the 'whosoever wills' (Revelation 22:17). If you want to be saved, come on! If you want to be saved, come to Jesus. He is reaching out His nail-pierced hands to you and saying, 'Come; come; come!'"[139]—Adrian Rogers

The heart of the Hyper-Calvinist movement in the church essentially states that Christ did not make provision for all men to be saved; He died to save just some. Such a belief is a smack in the face to John 3:16, which records, "For God so loved the world, that He gave His only begotten Son, that whoever believes in Him shall not perish, but have eternal life" (NASB). This text makes clear that God, through His Son Jesus Christ, made provision for all in the world to be saved (1 John 2:2; John 1:29). Further, Hyper-Calvinists embrace beliefs of irresistible grace, that all divinely elected to be saved cannot resist salvation, and limited atonement, that those not divinely elected (chosen) cannot be saved. In 2 Peter 3:9, God makes crystal clear His desire to save every man from Hell unto Heaven. "The Lord is not slack concerning his promise, as some men count slackness; but is longsuffering to us-ward, not willing that any should perish, but that all should come to repentance." Paul declared that we are to pray for "all men...For this is good and acceptable in the sight of God our Savior; Who will have ALL MEN to be saved, and to come unto the knowledge of the truth" (1 Timothy 2:1, 3–4). "I do not see," Adrian Rogers stated, "where it [the Bible] teaches God preselects some to salvation and consigns the rest of humanity to eternal damnation without ever making them a sincere offer of forgiveness."[140] Neither do I. Bruce R. Cole surmises: "Man is free to accept or reject Christ's offer of salvation, apart from any decision or coercion from the Godhead. 'Whosoever will' may be saved."[141]

God votes for us, Satan votes against us, and we cast the deciding ballot. Realizing this statement may oversimplify the doctrine of election, it nonetheless hits the crux of the issue. Salvation always has been and will remain a "whosoever will may come" proposition.

A danger of Hyper-Calvinism is that since it advocates Christ died to save only some, not all, effort to win the unsaved stops. After all, if it is a done deal, already decided by God who goes to Heaven and to Hell, personal evangelism is futile; thus, missionaries traveling to the uttermost parts of the world proclaiming the Gospel, as well as local personal evangelistic efforts, become unnecessary.

ASK YOURSELF

What Scripture supports the fact that God has made provision for all men to be saved?

Why do you believe or not believe that God has given man free will to choose to accept or reject Christ?

What view would you have of God, if, as the Hyper-Calvinists suggest, He predestined some to Heaven and others to Hell?

If you held to this view, how would it impact witnessing?

Chapter 14 The Trinitarian View of God

"Go ye therefore, and teach all nations, baptizing them in the name of the Father, and of the Son, and of the Holy Ghost."—Mathew 28:19.

"The Trinity is complicated, but not contradictory or illogical."[142]—Alex McFarland

Christians believe in one God, but this God exists in three Persons (Trinity). These three share one nature and are God the Father, God the Son, and God the Holy Spirit simultaneously. Christians call this the Trinity. D. L. Moody compared the Trinity to a triangle which is one figure, yet with three different sides at the same time. Patrick of Ireland used a shamrock to explain the Trinity. Holding up a shamrock, he would ask people, "Is it one leaf or three?" to which they would reply, "It is both one leaf and three." "And it is so with God," he would conclude.

"That the three members of the Trinity," states Norman Geisler, "are distinct persons [yet one] is clear in that each is mentioned in distinction from the others. The Son prayed to the Father (John 17). The Father spoke from Heaven about the Son at his baptism (Matthew 3:15–17). Indeed, the Holy Spirit was present at the same time, revealing that they coexist. Further, the fact that they have separate titles (Father, Son, and Spirit) indicates that they are not one Person. Also, each member of the Trinity has special functions that help us to identify them. For example, the Father planned salvation (John 3:16; Eph. 1:4), the Son accomplished it on the cross (John 17:4; 19:30; Heb. 1:1–2) and at the resurrection (Rom. 4:25; 1 Cor. 15:1–6), and the Holy Spirit applies it to the lives of the believers (John 3:5; Eph. 4:30; Titus 3:5–7). The Son submits to the Father (1 Cor. 11:3; 15:28), and the Holy Spirit glorifies the Son (John 16:14)."[143]

Objections to the Doctrine of the Trinity

The word Trinity is not found in Scripture.

Although the word "Trinity" does not occur in the Bible, the Trinitarian doctrine is revealed in texts such as Genesis 1:26; 3:22; Numbers 6:24–26; Isaiah 48:16; Matthew 28:19; 2 Corinthians 13:14; Luke 1:35; John 14:25–31; Galatians 4:6; 1 Peter 1:2; 1 John 5:6–8; Jude 20–21; Revelation 1:4–6. This doctrine is presented in Scripture but not explained. It is authenticated overwhelmingly.

If the Trinity (God, Jesus, Holy Spirit, one entity) is true, then why did Jesus pray to Himself in the Garden?

He did not pray to Himself in the garden, but to the Father. John MacArthur offers insight. "The Scriptures are clear that these three Persons together are one and only one God (Deut. 6:4). John 10:30 and 33 explain that the Father and the Son are one. First Corinthians 3:16 shows that the Father and the Spirit are one. Romans 8:9 makes clear that the Son and the Spirit are one. And John 14:16, 18, and 23 demonstrate that the Father, Son, and Spirit are one. Yet, in exhibiting the unity between the members of the Trinity, the Word of God in no way denies the simultaneous existence and distinctiveness of each of the three Persons of the Godhead. In other words, the Bible makes it clear that God is one God (not three), but that the one God is a Trinity of Persons."[144]

Mathematically, Father, Son, and Holy Spirit add up to three gods.

Norman Geisler responds, "Critics make a point of computing the mathematical impossibility of believing there are a Father, Son, and Holy Spirit in the Godhead without holding that there are three gods. Does not 1+1+1=3? It certainly does, if you add them; but Christians insist that the triunity of God is more like 1x1x1=1. God is triune, not triplex. His one essence has multiple centers of personhood. Thus, there is no more mathematical problem in conceiving the Trinity than there is in understanding 1 cubed (1 to the third power)."[145]

John 14:28 seems to indicate that Jesus is inferior to the Father.

Jesus meant in this text that the Father is greater in *office.*[146] Scripture makes clear that the Father, Son, and Holy Spirit are equal in authority and power. They do not work independently of the other, because they are "one in essence."[147]

The Trinity just doesn't compute; it doesn't make sense.

Many things which don't make sense are nonetheless true. To scientists, it doesn't make sense that a bumble bee can fly, but it does. C. S. Lewis makes a great point in stating, "If Christianity was something we were making up, of course we could make it easier. But it is not. We cannot compete in simplicity with people who are inventing religions. How could we? We are dealing with fact. Of course anyone can be simple if he has no facts to bother about."[148] "'My thoughts are nothing like your thoughts,' says the LORD. 'And my ways are far beyond anything you could imagine'" (Isaiah 55:8, NLT). With the finite mind, we cannot comprehend fully a God that is one Being existing coequally and coeternally as three Persons, but we can apprehend it through the Scripture and faith.[149]

Augustine was walking by the sea when he noticed a young boy building a trench in the sand. Approaching the young boy, he asked what he was doing. The boy replied, "I'm going to empty the sea into my trench." This great Latin thinker continued to walk and muse and said to himself, *So the lad thinks that he's going to empty the sea into the little trench he's made in the sand.* "Sometimes," he says, "we are like that. We propose to encompass the infinitude of God in the small limits of our minds. It cannot be achieved. It is impossible."[150] Christians certainly identify with Augustine. It's totally impossible to empty the sea (the scope and meaning of the Trinity) into the small trench of our finite minds.

ASK YOURSELF

What is the Trinity?

How might the Trinity be illustrated?

How might you respond to the statement, "The Trinity doesn't make sense"?

How can you understand the Trinity better?

Respond to the statement, "Mathematically, Father, Son, and Holy Spirit add up to three gods."

Explain Norman Geisler's statement: "There is only one 'What' (essence of God), but there are three 'Whos' in that one 'What.'"[151]

Chapter 15 The Existence of Satan

"Be sober, be vigilant; because your adversary the devil, as a roaring lion, walketh about, seeking whom he may devour."—1 Peter 5:8 .

"There are two equal and opposite errors into which our race can fall about the devils. One is to disbelieve in their existence. The other is to believe and to feel an excessive and unhealthy interest in them. They themselves are equally pleased by both errors."[152]—C. S. Lewis

Satan is for real. The primary witness to the reality and existence of Satan is not experience or even the repulsive, shameful, perverted, depraved and degenerate acts of man, but the testimony of Scripture. Both the Old Testament and New Testament unequivocally affirm Satan's reality.

"Satan" and "the Devil" are not simply names symbolizing evil and wrongdoing in the world. Satan is not a mythological character. Satan is not the comical caricature of one dressed in a red suit and bearing horns, a pitchfork and a tail. He is alive and well on planet earth. W. A. Criswell dramatically emphasizes this truth. "He is called by his name 174 times in the Word of God. He's called Satan. He's called the Devil. He's called that old serpent. He's called the dragon. He's called Beelzebub....[H]e is presented as a person, a personality, as somebody—like God is somebody, like Michael is somebody, like Gabriel is somebody. This enemy of ours *is* somebody. Eve met him in the Garden of Eden. Job had to do with him. He fell into the hands of Satan....Christ himself addressed him as Satan: 'Satan, get behind me!'—a personal enemy."[153]

Lucifer was an anointed cherub of God (Ezekiel 28:14) who, because of his extreme pride, rebelled against God. After falling from his high position (Isaiah 14:12), he became known as Satan. He possesses intelligence (2 Corinthians 2:11), memory (Matthew 4:6), a will (2 Timothy 2:26), a desire (Luke 22:31), wrath (Revelation

12:12), and great organizational ability (1 Timothy 4:1; Revelation 2:9, 24). His purpose is to usurp God's authority in the world by deceiving, lying, tempting, and destroying (John 10:10). Unlike God, though, Satan is not omnipresent. He is not everywhere at once. He employs countless demons ("unclean spirits," "evil spirits," "deceiving spirits") throughout the earth to antagonize and attack the believer (Matthew 10:1; Acts 19:12–13; 1 Timothy 4:1; Revelation 16:14). But the believer is promised victory over Satan's tactics (1 John 4:4). Some of Jesus' primary reasons for coming to earth were to overthrow Satan, neutralize his power (Matthew 12:25–29; John 12:31), and cast him and his demons into eternal damnation in the Lake of Fire and Brimstone (Matthew 25:41; Revelation 20:10). Knowing this about Jesus' plan for Satan helps our understanding of Hell. God created Hell for Satan and his demons, not for mankind. Nevertheless, anyone who lives alienated from God in rebellion and unbelief will suffer this eternal punishment. Yet God longs for all to be saved so that no one experiences the torment of Hell.

Satan is the originator of sin and evil. Donald Grey Barnhouse states in *The Invisible War*:

"The next verse in Ezekiel's account [chapter 28] gives us the key to the origin of evil in this universe. 'Thou wast perfect in thy ways from the day that thou wast created, till iniquity was found in thee' (verse 15). What this iniquity was is revealed to us in some detail in the prophecy of Isaiah, but there are already interesting indications in our passage that we may not pass by. The fact given here is that iniquity came by what we might term spontaneous generation in the heart of this being in whom such magnificence of power and beauty had been combined and to whom such authority and privilege had been given. Here is the beginning of sin. Iniquity was found in the heart of Lucifer. So far as we know, here is the only verse in the Bible which states clearly the exact origin of sin. Other passages only amplify this one; for instance, the passage we will consider later when we come to the nature of man's sin and what we might call the rules under which sin is practiced (Isaiah 45:7). But the passage before us is the stark declaration by God that sin originated in the heart of Lucifer."[154]

The schemes of Satan, of which he is author, manifest his presence in the world:

- Lying (John 8:44);

- Tempting (Matthew 4:1);

- Robbing (Matthew 13:19);

- Harassing (2 Corinthians 12:7);

- Hindering (1 Thessalonians 2:18);

- Sifting (Luke 22:31);

- Imitating (2 Corinthians 11:14–15);

- Accusing (Revelation 12:9–10);

- Smiting with disease (Luke 13:16);

- Possessing (John 13:27);

- Killing and devouring (John 8:44).

As if the accounts of Satan and his work were not enough to make clear the reality of his influence in the world, Scripture also assigns an array of descriptive names and titles to our opponent:

- Satan—the opposer (Matthew 4:10, Rev. 12:9; 20:2);

- Devil—the accuser (Matthew 4:1, Ephesians 4:27);

- Lucifer—the shining one (Isaiah 14:12; 2 Cor. 11:14);

- Anointed cherub—the lofty ranking among angels which he held prior to his fall (Ezekiel 28:14);

- Evil one—the personification of evil (Matthew 13:19, 38; John 17:15);

- Ruler of this world—the one who presides over the evil world system of men and demons; Jesus called Satan this three times (John 12:31; 14:30; 16:11);

- God of this age—the blinder of minds regarding the Gospel (2 Corinthians 4:4);

- Prince of the power of the air—the pervasive one (John 12:31; Ephesians 2:2);

- Serpent—the deceiving and devious one (Genesis 3:1; 2 Corinthians 11:3);

- Dragon—the fiercest one possessing power to destroy (Revelation 12:3, 7–9);

- Accuser—the accuser of the saint before God (Revelation 12:10);

- Deceiver—the counterfeiter of truth and right (Revelation 12:9; 20:3);

- Murderer—the one who brought death to Adam and the whole human race (John 8:44; Genesis 3:1–7);

- Liar—the wellspring of untruth (John 8:44);

- Sinner—the first sinner (1 John 3:8);

- Beelzebub—the ruler of a demonic host (Matthew 10:25; 12:24, 27; Luke 11:15);

- Belial—the "worthless" or "wicked" one (2 Corinthians 6:15);

- Roaring lion—the hungry evil one whose appetite devours the believer (1 Peter 5:8).

Satan does exist, but he tries to conceal his reality. "And it is no wonder, for Satan himself masquerades as an angel of light; so it is not surprising if his servants also masquerade as ministers of righteousness. [But] their end will correspond with their deeds" (2 Corinthians 11:14–15, Amplified). In the *Screwtape Letters,* authored by C. S. Lewis, the demon Screwtape instructs an apprentice to do just this very thing:

"I wonder you should ask me whether it is essential to keep the patient in ignorance of your own existence. That question, at least for the present phase of the struggle, has been answered for us by the High Command. Our policy, for the moment, is to conceal ourselves. Of course this has not always been so. We are really faced with a cruel dilemma. When the humans disbelieve in our existence, we lose all the pleasing results of direct terrorism, and we make no magicians. On the other hand, when they believe in us, we cannot make them materialists and skeptics—at least, not yet. I have great hopes that we shall learn in due time how to emotionalize and mythologize their science to such an extent that what is, in effect, belief in us (though not under that name) will creep in while the human mind remains closed to belief in the Enemy. The 'Life Force,' the worship of sex, and some aspects of Psychoanalysis may here prove useful. If once we can produce our perfect work—the Materialist Magician, the man, not using, but veritably worshipping, what he vaguely calls 'Forces' while denying the existence of 'spirits'—then the end of the war will be in sight. But in the meantime, we must obey our orders. I do not think you will have much difficulty in keeping the patient in the dark. The fact that 'devils' are predominantly comic figures in the modern imagination will help you. If any faint suspicion of your existence begins to arise in his mind, suggest to him a picture of something in red tights, and persuade him that since he cannot believe in that (it is an old textbook method of confusing them), he therefore cannot believe in you."[155]

"The devil is delighted to be denied!" states Jack R. Taylor. "He doesn't want to be given credit for a job well done! He resists detection. He doesn't desire your consideration....But remember, you cannot defeat an enemy as long as you deny him. Face the foe! Find out who he is! Force him to acknowledge the truth! Fight the fight of faith and watch him FLEE!"[156] A man came to Charles Finney, the well-known evangelist, and said, "I don't believe in the existence of a devil."

"Don't you?" asked Finney. "Well, you resist him for a while, and you will believe in it."

The Existence of Satan

State why you do not believe that Satan is a mythological character or figment of one's imagination.

What is the biblical evidence of Satan's existence?

What point did C. S. Lewis make in the reference cited from *The Screwtape Letters,* and how valid is it?

In what ways does Satan masquerade?

Who is the originator of sin and evil?

Do you believe that Satan is a "he" (personality) or an impersonal force? Why?

What are some of the works of Satan?

Chapter 16 Absolute Truth

"I am the way, the truth and the life."—John 14:6.

Do fixed, unalterable and invariable facts exist? Are standards of right and wrong and concepts like truth and error regarding morals, ethics, and faith valid universally? Is one truth as good as another? Is there absolute truth in the world?

There are two differing views to these questions. Relativism espouses the view that there is no absolute truth to define reality, that everything is relative to something else. In essence, relativism states that the rightness or wrongness of an action all depends on the circumstances or situation (situation ethics); if it feels good and right at the moment, then it's okay to do it. It is this philosophy that embraces the view that since there is no absolute truth (for every man decides that for himself based on the situation), then all values, beliefs and lifestyles are equally valid. The other view (Christian) emphatically claims there are fixed standards and realities (absolute truth) to govern man's belief and behavior, clearly identifying what is right and wrong.

Regarding relativism, Josh McDowell states, "What if there is a God out there, a God who is the only source of certainty, meaning, purpose, and identity? And what if, as Christianity affirms, there is only one road by which you can reach Him and that is through a relationship with the person of Jesus Christ? What would that do to the notion that we should affirm all beliefs as valid? It would kill it."[157] McDowell continues, "If there is one solid absolute truth, then the idea that we can create our own truth is fatal. It is the most dangerous doctrine we can adopt, because if you hold to a belief that does not exist as an objective reality, you are in jeopardy of missing out on the promises and benefits of knowing the real God."[158]

"While people may say, 'Don't impose your beliefs on me,' you never hear them say, 'Don't impose your mathematics on me.'

Why don't we say that? Because we assume math is connected to reality. In math, answers are either right or wrong, and it's the same with moral and spiritual beliefs."[159]

The Bible Is Absolute Truth

The gigantic shift among Christian students regarding fixed, unalterable and invariable facts (91% of born-again students reject absolute truth[160]) is due to weakened belief regarding God and the Bible. Obviously, to believe that one religion is as good as another or one standard of morals is as good as another, though it differs vastly, and to embrace situation ethics is to deny God's sovereignty and the Bible's implicit authority.

Adrian Rogers aptly stated, "Satan's chief weapon is deception. The Devil would rather peddle a lie than a barrel of whiskey or a kilo of illegal drugs any day. Satan would rather get you to believe a wrong thing than to do a wrong thing. He is the sinister minister of destruction. Why? Because a lie is the most dangerous thing on the face of the earth. It is antithetical to God, who is Truth and whose Word is truth (John 17:17). Satan is a pusher of lies, because the thought is the father of the deed."[161] Relativism (no absolutes), subjectivism (what truth is to you), pragmatism (truth determined by whether it works or not), and postmodernism (there is no truth) are all lies Satan is pushing.

Commenting on Psalm 119, C. H. Spurgeon said, "What is truth? The holy Scriptures are the only answer to that question. Note that they are not only true, but *the truth* itself. We may not say of them that they contain the truth, but that they *are* the truth: 'Thy law is the truth.' There is nothing false about the law or preceptory part of Scripture. Those who are obedient thereto shall find that they are walking in a way consistent with fact, while those who act contrary thereto are walking in a vain show."[162]

John Calvin wrote, "This is the principle that distinguishes our religion from all others, that we know that God has spoken to us and are fully convinced that the prophets did not speak of themselves but, as organs of the Holy Spirit, uttered only that which they had been commissioned from Heaven to declare. All those who wish to profit from the Scriptures must first accept this as a settled principle, that the law and the prophets are not teachings handed on at pleasure of men or produced by men's minds as their source, but are dictated by the Holy Spirit. We owe to the Scriptures the same reverence as we owe to God, since it has its only source in Him and has nothing of human origin mixed with it."[163]

To one who accepts the divine inspiration (God authorship) of the Bible, the reality of absolute truth is forever settled. (See Hot Buttons 1–3 on the credibility of the Bible.) The Bible is the moral and theological code book for the entire world. Its teachings are truth, trustworthy for all mankind's acceptance and adherence (John 10:35). It is the sole standard, measuring rod, plumb line that dictates right and wrong, truth and error.

A good question to ask those who say there is no absolute truth is, "Are you absolutely sure of that?" If they answer, "Yes," they have made an absolute statement, which implies the existence of absolute truth. In essence, they have countered their own claim.

ASK YOURSELF

What are the two primary views regarding absolute truth; cite their differences?

What legitimate reason is there for embracing the Christian view of absolute truth?

Cite the danger, according to McDowell, that exists in embracing the view of relativism.

Explain the statement, "If you accept the inspiration of the Bible, then you will embrace Absolute Truth."

What question might you ask another who emphatically states the nonexistence of absolute truth?

List some absolute truths.

Chapter 17   Is Jesus the Only Savior?

"Jesus saith unto him, I am the way, the truth, and the life: no man cometh unto the Father, but by me."—John 14:6.

Is Jesus the only Savior? Pluralists would say, "No." Pluralists are persons who believe that Jesus is the provision of God for salvation, but that "there are other ways of getting right with God and gaining eternal bliss in other religions. The work of Christ is useful for Christians but not essential for non-Christians."[164]

Exclusivists would say emphatically, "Yes" to the stated question, which is the traditional view of the evangelical church. Exclusivists (evangelical Christians) base such belief upon the Holy Scripture, which clearly and forthrightly asserts that salvation is solely in, of and through Jesus Christ (conscious knowledge and acceptance of Jesus through faith and repentance.) Adrian Rogers well speaks for evangelical Christians: "Somehow, in the matter that matters the most—our eternal destiny—people say, 'Well, it just doesn't matter what you believe. All roads lead to Heaven.' No, they do not. There is one Gospel, and it is the Gospel of the grace of God."[165]

New Testament References Substantiate the Belief That There Is One Way, Jesus as Savior

"For God so loved the world, that he gave his only begotten Son, that whosoever believeth in him should not perish, but have everlasting life. For God sent not his Son into the world to condemn the world; but that the world through him might be saved. He that believeth on him is not condemned: but he that believeth not is condemned already, because he hath not believed in the name of the only begotten Son of God" (John 3:16–18).

"Jesus saith unto him, I am the way, the truth, and the life: no man cometh unto the Father, but by me" (John 14:6).

"I am the door: by me if any man enter in, he shall be saved, and shall go in and out, and find pasture" (John 10:9).

It is impossible to misunderstand or misinterpret the truth revealed by Jesus in these passages. He plainly states that salvation (reconciliation to God) is possible only in and through Him. The Book of Acts sounds the same note in declaring, "Be it known unto you all, and to all the people of Israel, that by the name of Jesus Christ of Nazareth, whom ye crucified, whom God raised from the dead, even by him doth this man stand here before you whole. This is the stone which was set at nought of you builders, which is become the head of the corner. Neither is there salvation in any other: for there is none other name under heaven given among men, whereby we must be saved" (Acts 4:10–12). The apostle Paul said, "For there is only one God and one Mediator who can reconcile God and humanity—the man Christ Jesus" (1 Timothy 2:5 NLT). There is not one door to salvation for the Baptists and another for the Buddhists, one for the Methodists and another for the Mormons, one for the Presbyterians and another for the Pentecostals. There is but one door to Heaven, and that is the Lord Jesus Christ. All who will be saved must embrace faith in the Lord Jesus Christ alone.

The Committee on Evangelical Unity in the Gospel press statement summarizes the evangelical Christian's belief on the acquisition of salvation: "The heart of the Gospel is that our holy, loving Creator, confronted with human hostility and rebellion, has chosen in His own freedom and faithfulness to become our holy, loving Redeemer and Restorer. The Father has sent the Son to be the Savior of the world (1 John 4:14); it is through His one and only Son that God's one and only plan of salvation is implemented."[166]

ASK YOURSELF

Contrast the two views regarding the way to salvation?

Is it possible for a person to be saved by some other means than through the atoning work of Jesus Christ on the Cross? Why or why not?

Are believers who embrace exclusivism narrow-minded regarding their stance on salvation?

How might you counter the argument of the pluralist?

Chapter 18 How Is One Saved?

"For by grace are ye saved through faith; and that not of yourselves: it is the gift of God: Not of works, lest any man should boast."—Ephesians 2:8, 9.

H. A. Ironside wrote, "While presenting the Gospel on the street of a California city, we were often interrupted about as follows: 'Look here, sir! There are hundreds of religions in this country, and the followers of each sect think theirs is the only right one. How can poor, plain men like us find out what really is the truth?' We generally replied something like this: 'Hundreds of religions, you say? That's strange; I've heard of only two.' 'Oh, but you surely know there are more than that?' 'Not at all, sir. I find, I admit, many shades of difference in the opinions of those comprising the two great schools; but, after all, there are but two. The one covers all who expect salvation by doing; the other, all who have been saved by something done. So you see the whole question is very simple. Can you save yourself, or must you be saved by another? If you can be your own savior, you do not need my message. If you cannot, you may well listen to it.'"[167] Ironside is right. There are basically only two *religious* views regarding the manner in which man is saved. One advocates works; the other, grace.

The Bible teaches that the only way to be saved is by grace through faith in the Lord Jesus Christ. Salvation is a gift to be received, not a reward to be earned. Christianity isn't a list of things to do. It is a relationship made possible through what Christ has done. Man is saved by Jesus' work, not his own. This fact alone differentiates Christianity from the religions of the world. "You can't buy it, borrow it, steal it, or earn it," declares Adrian Rogers. Rogers continues, "It is grace of God, and it was bought by Christ on the cross. Friend, when He finished, it was accomplished, and you cannot deplete it or add to it—it is the supernatural work of God. Salvation is not a creed. You're not saved by the *plan* of salvation; you're saved by the *Man* of salvation. It's not a cause or a church. It's Christ. We have so much religious mayhem in the world today because people have met creeds, not Christ. They've entered into codes of living, but not Christ. They join churches without meeting Christ. Salvation is not believing something; it is receiving Someone."[168]

C. H. Spurgeon, speaking against works' involvement in salvation, said, "If there is one stitch in the celestial garment of my righteousness which I am to insert, then I am lost." Man's imperfect state disqualifies him to have anything to do with his reconciliation to God. "We are all infected and impure with sin. When we display our righteous deeds, they are nothing but filthy rags. Like autumn leaves, we wither and fall, and our sins sweep us away like the wind" (Isaiah 64:6 NLT). "If we were responsible for our own salvation," declares John Stott, "either in whole or even in part, we would be justified in singing our own praises and blowing our own trumpet in Heaven. But such a thing is inconceivable. God's redeemed people will spend eternity worshipping Him, humbling themselves before Him in grateful adoration, ascribing their salvation to Him and to the Lamb, and acknowledging that He alone is worthy to receive all praise, honor and glory. Why? Because our salvation is due entirely to His grace, will, initiative, wisdom and power."[169] Salvation is all of Jesus Christ or not at all.

A salvation by grace without works is too easy for some to accept. Like Naaman the leper, they feel what is told them to do to be saved is too simple; surely it requires keeping the command-ments, religious deeds and a moral life (2 Kings 5:11–19). But the Bible says it is not so (Ephesians 2:8–9). A cake mix company promoted its product as requiring nothing but water to be added by the housewife to make a creamy and delicious cake. It did not sell. Marketing research discovered the reason for its failure was that the public felt uneasy about a mix that required only water to be added. It seemed too simple. The public felt they had to do more personally in making the cake batter. The company changed the cake formula, requiring an egg to be added. Immediately sales soared.[170] Sadly, far too many feel this same way about salvation.

Peter wrote, "Ye were not redeemed with corruptible things, [like] silver and gold...but with the precious blood of Christ" (1 Pet. 1:18–19). The writer of Hebrews says, "Without shedding of blood is no remission" (Hebrews 9:22). The literal shed blood of Jesus, His sacrificial death upon the Cross, was necessary to satisfy the demand of the law making possible man's salvation. Jesus the Just took the place of man the unjust; Jesus the sinless took the place of the sinful, paying the price for sin not His own (substitutionary death). This was the means that God ordained, for Christ to die to make possible man's forgiveness and reconciliation unto Himself. What awesome love was on display when Jesus suffered upon the cross the most excruciating form of death known to the world to save sinners like you and me! It is a no-brainer that if man could have been saved by any other means than through Jesus' sacrificial death, the cross at Calvary would have been avoided.

Jesus Alone Both Could and Did Pay Our Sin Debt

Man owes a sin debt to God which he is unable to pay. Who qualifies to pay this debt for man?

To pay the sin debt, the payer would have to be capable of paying that kind of debt, capable of paying that large a debt, capable to take the place of man, sinless (without any debt), and be willing to pay the debt.[171] "To sum up these requirements," writes J. Budziszewski, "our debt against God could be paid only by a sinless human being who could count as a new representative of every human being, one who loved us so much that he was willing to spend himself for us—but who was also God, so that He could spend Himself without limit. In other words, God Himself would have to take the heat for us—as a man. And He did it."[172]

"The great superiority of the sacrifice Jesus brought," writes William Barclay, "lay in three things.

(1) The sacrifice of Jesus shows us a God whose arms are always outstretched and in whose heart is only love.

(2) The sacrifice of Jesus brought eternal redemption. The idea was that men were under the dominion of sin; and just as the purchase price had to be paid to free a man from slavery, so the purchase price had to be paid to free a man from sin.

(3) The sacrifice of Christ enabled a man to leave the deeds of death and to become the servant of the living God. That is to say, he did not only win forgiveness for a man's past sin; he enabled him in the future to live a godly life.

The sacrifice of Jesus was not only the paying of a debt; it was the giving of a victory. What Jesus did puts a man right with God, and what He does enables a man to stay right with God. The act of the cross brings to men the love of God in a way that takes their terror of Him away; the presence of the living Christ brings to them the power of God so that they can win a daily victory over sin."[173]

Ask Yourself

All religions boil down to offering one of two means for salvation; name and describe them.

Is the shed blood of Jesus necessary for man's salvation? Why or why not?

What is the "substitutionary death" of Jesus?

Why is Spurgeon's statement about man's merit or works having no role in salvation true?

In what three ways is the sacrifice of Jesus superior to that of animals in the Old Testament?

In what five ways did Jesus alone qualify to pay man's sin debt against God?

In what way are some people like Naaman?

Chapter 19 What about Those Who Never Heard the Gospel?

"For the wrath of God is revealed from heaven against all ungodliness and unrighteousness of men, who hold the truth in unrighteousness; Because that which may be known of God is manifest in them; for God hath shewed it unto them. For the invisible things of him from the creation of the world are clearly seen, being understood by the things that are made, even his eternal power and Godhead; so that they are without excuse."—Romans 1:18–20.

The question of the eternal fate of the heathen who never hear the gospel message is an issue with which all evangelical Christians wrestle at some juncture and one which the gainsayers often bring up. Our head tells us one thing; our heart tells us another about their judgment and eternal abode. As with all other issues, the Christian must stick to the knowledge available on the subject (Holy Scripture) and refrain from mere speculation. What is the outcome for those who never hear the Gospel proclaimed?

In Romans 1:18–20, the Apostle Paul cites that the heathen are without excuse, because they have received the light of creation (evidence of the Creator abounds in the universe) and the conscience (right and wrong are internally known). This light ought to lead people to seek out more light (information) regarding God and reconciliation to Him, like the Ethiopian Eunuch (Acts 8:26–31) and Cornelius (Acts 10:1–6) did. Rejection of the revealed light or failure to use the light to seek more information about God blocks further revelation, which includes the gospel message. This is why man is without excuse. Adrian Rogers stated, "God gives us truth; when we believe that truth, God gives us more truth. Light obeyed increases light. God speaks to us through creation and conscience; we respond to God, 'I want to know You; I need to know You,' and God gives more light. If we do not believe in or trust in God when He gives us light (speaks to our hearts through creation and conscience), then we will begin to regress and lose even the light that we have."[174]

Let me illustrate the point. Imagine being hopelessly lost deep in the forest at midnight, when all of a sudden a shining light appears in the far distance. You have one of two options—ignore the light or walk toward the light. Opting to walk toward the light, you learn that the closer to the light you come, the brighter it appears, lighting up the path to rescue. In order to be rescued, you have to act upon what "light" is present (though perhaps faint at the start) until it becomes full-flamed. This is the argument the Apostle Paul is making in Romans 1 regarding the heathen. God is fair and just and merciful to all, not willing that any should perish. He is shining the light in man's spiritual darkness of eternal lostness, pointing the way to salvation through Christ, but man must act upon that light if he is to be saved (Acts 4:12). Robert Mounce states, "No one is excluded. No one can get away with saying, 'I don't believe in God.' As someone has said, 'You can't turn out the light by closing your eyes.' The heathen who has never heard the Gospel or the name of Jesus is as responsible as anyone else—not for failing to accept a message he has never heard, but for rejecting the knowledge of God revealed in creation. People do not suffer eternal exclusion from God for not having been born to the right parents in the right part of the world, but for rejecting that knowledge of God which is readily available for all."[175]

If it were possible for the heathen to be saved apart from reception of the gospel message, then missionaries do them a grave injustice in proclaiming it to them. R. C. Sproul explains: "The unspoken assumption [an assumption he does not embrace] at this point is that the only damnable offense against God is rejection of Christ. Since the native is not guilty of this, we ought to leave him alone. In fact, leaving him alone would be the most helpful thing we could do for him. If we go to the native and inform him of Christ, we place his soul in eternal jeopardy, for now he knows of Christ, and if he refuses to respond to Him, he can no longer claim ignorance as an excuse. Hence, the best service we can render is silence."[176] If this view is correct, then let's burn all the Bibles, shut down the churches, recall the missionaries, and never utter the name of Christ, so everybody may be "saved." Obviously, the unspoken assumption is unscriptural and thus incorrect.

The same note is emphasized by Bill Cashion, former missionary, in response to another who believed the untold of the world would be saved due to their ignorance. "You have created the 'gospel of ignorance,' and according to you, it is more powerful than the Gospel of the cross. According to your "gospel," all that needs to be done to be forgiven and to enter Heaven is to stay away from the Gospel of Jesus Christ. If that is true, then we have two major complaints with God: 1) if ignorance is all that is required to be saved, why didn't God just leave all of us alone, allow us to enjoy this season of sin called life, and then take us all to Heaven; 2) if ignorance is all that is required, why would we even want to know and worship a God who would take Heaven's best, His only Son, and sentence Him to a cruel and torturous death on the cross, if that death was unnecessary and meaningless in the light of the power of 'ignorance'?"[177]

The rejection of Christ is a heinous sin—yea, the greatest sin—but only one of many which man commits. No one will go to Hell for failure to hear of Jesus Christ. Man goes to Hell for transgression of the Law (sin), of which all are guilty (Romans 3:23). It is man's sin that condemns him to Hell, not God (John 3:17–18). Thus man goes to Hell because he is a sinner, not because of failure to hear the gospel message. The rejection of Christ simply seals the unsaved sinner's fate.

Here is a farmer in Indonesia who is diagnosed with incurable cancer and is told by doctors to prepare for death. At the very moment he is told the bad news, a research hospital in the United States discovers the cure for the man's type of cancer. But the hospital knows nothing of the man, nor does the man know of the hospital. In time the man dies. Why? He dies because he has cancer, not because he didn't get the cure. Not getting the cure simply sealed his fate. The world has been diagnosed with the cancer of sin and is terminally ill. A cure was made available 2,000 years ago by God. The cure is the spilt blood of Jesus Christ (1 John 1:7–8) which has the power to cure the worst of sinners. Sadly, many are unaware of the cure and will die an eternal death (Hell). Why? Not because they never heard the Good News of divine remedy, but because of the cancer of sin. Not hearing the gospel message simply seals their eternal doom.[178]

It is explicitly clear in Scripture that there is only one means by which a person may be saved (justified, made right with God, inherit Heaven), and that means is Jesus Christ (John 10:9; 14:6). God only promised salvation for individuals who exhibit repentance and faith in the Lord Jesus Christ (Acts 20:21; Luke 13:3; Romans 10:17; Romans 10:13). The Great Commission and Acts 1:8 both would be unnecessary if man might be saved apart from conscious reception of Jesus Christ. These texts pungently make clear the Christian's responsibility to be missionary in practice and purse (God's lights locally and globally) reaching the untold 1.6 billion with the Gospel.

"In His love and mercy," writes William Lane Craig, "God ensures that no one who would believe the Gospel if he heard it is born at a time and place in history where he fails to hear it. Those who do not respond to God's general revelation in nature and conscience and never hear the Gospel would not respond to it if they did hear it. Hence, no one is lost because of historical or geographical accident. Anyone who wants or even would want to be saved will be saved."[179] I believe God will by some means get the message of the Gospel to every person, regardless of geographical remoteness, who wants to be saved, just like was the case with the Ethiopian Eunuch and Cornelius. Missionaries attest to this very truth. Rest assured that the God of the Universe will do what is just and fair, according to His divine nature and Word, with all people.

C. S. Lewis stated, "In the meantime, if you are worried about the people outside, the most unreasonable thing you can do is to remain outside yourself. Christians are Christ's body, the organism through which He works….If you want to help those outside, you must add your own little cell to the body of Christ, who alone can help them."[180] Bill Cashion capsulizes the issue regarding those who have yet to hear the Gospel. "You are asking the wrong question. Everywhere I go, people ask, 'What about those who have never heard?' The Bible does not ask this question. Our Lord told us 2,000 years ago to go into all the world and preach the Gospel to every creature, and we still have not obeyed His command. So, in light of His command, the question the Bible asks is: 'What about those of us who have heard, believed, but have never shared?'"[181]

ASK YOURSELF

What light has God given all men since creation?

What role does this light play in ultimately bringing man to the knowledge of personal sin and need of reconciliation with God?

Is God just and fair by allowing the heathen who never heard of Christ to go to Hell?

What is the unasked assumption?

What is it that condemns a person to Hell? What is the only means of salvation?

Why was the Great Commission issued by our Lord?

What is meant by Adrian Rogers' statement: "Light increases light"?

Chapter 20   The Authority of the Bible

"I have used Apollos and myself as examples so you could learn through us the meaning of the saying, 'Follow only what is written in the Scriptures.'"—1 Corinthians 4:6 NCV.

In response to a critical and egoistical attack on his credibility, the Apostle Paul, in essence, said to his accusers, "It's not man's evaluation of my life and ministry, or mine, that matters, but that of Holy Scripture, which is the criterion for belief and conduct." Based upon this statement, observe several life-changing truths regarding the authority of the Word of God.

The Word overrules my conscience. Paul stated that his conscience didn't convict him of unfaithfulness or doctrinal error, but that didn't mean he was right. It was not the conscience that was to be his justifier, but the Word of God (verse 6). The fact the conscience does not sting regarding a sinful act does not justify the act. The Word of God always trumps the conscience. The conscience can only give guidance to the degree it is sanctified by the Holy Spirit and saturated with sound biblical doctrine. Don't let your conscience be your guide, but the written Word of God.

The Word overrules my companions. The Bible, not friends or family, has the authority to dictate right and wrong conduct. It's helpful at times to consult friends and family about choices in life, but never allow what they share to take precedence over the Word of God.

The Word overrules my culture. Mistakenly, some students allow their culture to dictate right and wrong practices. In today's culture, it is permissible, even expected, to engage in premarital sex, drink alcohol, shoot up heroin, devour pornography, cheat at school, dress immodestly, or have an abortion. But it is Christ, not culture, that is to guide us when we navigate lifestyle and choices. The Word of God trumps culture.

The Word overrules my convictions. Convictions must be anchored to sound biblical truth prior to implementation to be valid. Far too many embrace convictions that are not based on truth, resulting in warped values and injurious actions. Just because a person believes something to be true doesn't mean it is truth, nor does his rejection of something mean that it is an untruth (subjective believism). Truth is Truth, whether believed or not. What then is the source of Truth? Jesus answers, "I am the way, the truth, and the life: no man cometh unto the Father, but by me" (John 14:6). Theologian Clark Pinnock stated, "The claims of Christ are the cognitive informational facts upon which all historical, logical, and ordinary decisions are based."[182] God's Word is Truth. "There is nothing but truth in your word, and all of your righteous regulations endure forever" (Psalm 119:160 GWT). "Thy word is truth" (John 17:17). Never alter Scripture to adapt to convictions, but alter convictions to adjust to Scripture. The Word always trumps convictions.

The Word overrules my church. The church has no authority over the Bible. If the church advocates a position contrary to the teaching of Holy Scripture, always side with the Bible. The Word trumps the church.

In conclusion, how then can a person decide if a thing is right or wrong? Take the matter of abortion. Should it be decided by your conscience, companions, culture, conviction, or church? No, it can only be decided by the Word. Take the matter of premarital sex. Should it be decided by your conscience, companions, culture, conviction, or church? No, it can only be decided by the Word. Take the matter of alcohol and drug usage. Should it be decided by your conscience, companions, culture, conviction, or church? No, it can only be decided by the Word. Take the matter of pornography, homosexuality, or same-sex marriage. Should these be decided by your conscience, companions, culture, conviction, or church? No, they can only be decided by the Word. Take the matter of salvation? Should it be decided by your conscience, companions, culture, conviction, or church? No, it can only be decided by the Word. We may confidently declare with the Apostle Paul, "The Bible is the final authority on all matters, and I will obey what it states, regardless of opposition."

ASK YOURSELF

How valid is the statement, "Let your conscience be your guide?"

Has the conscience ever misguided you; and if so, in what way?

What kind of conscience can be trusted to lead rightly?

In regard to conduct, is the opinion of friends, culture trends, or church teaching the determining factor regarding what is acceptable or not?

If so, how does this attitude differ from that of the Apostle Paul?

Explain why living out one's convictions may lead to wrong acts.

What should supersede the conscience, companions, convictions, culture, and the church in determining right and wrong and how one ought to live?

Chapter 21 Tolerance or Compromise

"And Jesus went into the temple of God, and cast out all them that sold and bought in the temple, and overthrew the tables of the moneychangers, and the seats of them that sold doves."—Matthew 21:12.

"Ours is an age of tolerance. Men love to have the best of both worlds and hate to be forced to choose. It is commonly said that it does not matter what people believe so long as they are sincere, and that it is unwise to clarify issues too plainly or to focus them too sharply. But the religion of the New Testament is vastly different from this mental outlook. Christianity will not allow us to sit on the fence or live in a haze; it urges us to be definite and decisive."[183]—John Stott

Tolerance—you hear it mentioned often in the news and at school. What is it? Merriam-Webster Dictionary defines "tolerance" as "sympathy or indulgence for beliefs or practices differing from or conflicting with one's own." Many students have come to believe that absolute tolerance is politically correct and that immoral and deviant conduct is a personal choice not to be judged or jeopardized by God or man. This is an incorrect view of true tolerance. True tolerance has defined limits and is to be based upon what is morally pure and right instead of a broad stroke encompassing everything. Jesus certainly was not tolerant with evil deeds. How can a Christian justify tolerance for abortion, euthanasia, genocide, slavery, same-sex marriage, and spouse or child abuse, which are moral atrocities? Biblically and morally, he cannot. Intolerance (opposition) must always be garbed in the graciousness and sweetness of Christ—vocal but not violent, defiant but not demeaning, contradictory but not contemptuous, authoritative but not argumentative.

"Tolerance today," stated Adrian Rogers "is the great enemy of Christian purity. Tolerance puts a bend in the arrow that should not be there and gives it a blunt end. Tolerance in some matters is virtue, but the state religion today seems to be the religion of tolerance. No longer is it sufficient to 'love your neighbor.' Now our kids are taught, 'Not only must you love your neighbors, but you must tolerate all of his or her behavior. If you don't agree with that behavior, you must repent, because you are not to judge. Embrace all people and their behavior, or else you are the one that is wrong.' Only a fool would deny that tolerance can be a virtue. There are issues on which we should be open-minded, circumstances that require forbearance, and some areas in which we need to live and let live; but tolerance that calls for abandonment of conviction is of Hell!" Rogers further stated that "Tolerance is sometimes incompatible with basic truth."[184] G. K. Chesterton wisely said, "Tolerance is the virtue for those who do not believe much."[185]

A. W. Tozer declared, "There is a great hue and cry throughout the world today on behalf of tolerance, and much of it comes from a rising spirit of godlessness in the nations. The most intolerant nations and national leaders are preaching tolerance, calling for the breakdown of all barriers of religion and differences....[T]he Bible is the most intolerant book in all the world, and the most intolerant teacher that ever addressed Himself to an audience was the Lord Jesus Christ Himself. Now Jesus Christ demonstrated the vast difference between being charitable and being tolerant. Christ was so charitable that in His great heart, He was willing to weep over sinners; He took in all the people of the world and was willing to die for those who hated Him. But even with that kind of love and charity, Jesus was so intolerant that He taught, 'If you are not on my side, then you are against me; if you do not believe that I am He, you will die in your sins.' He did not leave any middle ground to accommodate the neutral folks who preach tolerance. Christ leaves no middle ground, no place in between."[186]

Toleration for impure, immoral, violent, and unethical acts stems from several sources.

A Person's Warped Theology.

"A truth perverted," states C. H. Spurgeon, "is generally worse than a doctrine which all know to be false."[187] The perversion of the truth obviously impacts one's views and practice.

A Person's Profane Lifestyle.

Desensitization to the wrongness of an act and thus favorable conviction toward it springs from its repetitive engagement. The prophet Isaiah warned, "Woe unto them that call evil good, and good evil; that put darkness for light, and light for darkness; that put bitter for sweet, and sweet for bitter" (Isaiah 5:20).

A Person's Delusion by Satan.

Some students have been brainwashed (subliminally in part) by the world (rock artists, Hollywood stars, politicians, liberal clergy, and culture) into acceptance of all forms of immoral conduct and affirmation of those who therein engage. In essence, they say, "It's not my thing, but its okay with me if it's your thing."

A Person's Cowardice.

"The person [who] never disagrees with anyone about anything even when they know that the other person is being incoherent or dishonest or simply false is not being tolerant but instead is a coward."[188] Sadly, too many students fit this characterization; fearful of the repercussions for voicing opposition, they remain quiet. A. W. Tozer, in *Love vs. Tolerance,* concluded, "So tolerance is a spreading disease that is eating away at the absolutes of divine revelation and the unchanging truths of the Bible. But tolerance must not be tolerated by the true Christian, even when it costs them misunderstanding or alienation from friends, family, and this world."[189]

Intolerance, not tolerance of evil, is the compassionate attitude. Voicing disapproval of a lifestyle that will bear hurtful and perhaps deadly consequences individually (and possibly for others) is far superior to affirming behavior without concern for the person's well-being. Knowing the fruit of sin, Jesus condemned it and compelled man to turn from it. As His disciples, we can do no less.

ASK YOURSELF

What is the dangerous trend of tolerance in student circles?

Cite the four sources for tolerance of evil?

Explain how tolerance of evil may be simply a shroud to hide cowardice.

What might Adrian Rogers mean in stating that "tolerance that calls for abandonment of conviction is of Hell!"?

How is intolerance of evil a more compassionate attitude than that of tolerance?

What is the criterion for deciding an attitude of tolerance or intolerance toward an issue or practice (Ephesians 5:11)?

How is the Christian to express intolerance?

Honestly, are you a casualty of mental subliminal suggestion or other worldly means of indoctrination to the degree that tolerance of wrong is seen as politically and morally correct?

Is this still your belief?

Chapter 22 A Biblical Worldview

"I beseech you therefore, brethren, by the mercies of God, that ye present your bodies a living sacrifice, holy, acceptable unto God, which is your reasonable service. And be not conformed to this world: but be ye transformed by the renewing of your mind, that ye may prove what is that good, and acceptable, and perfect, will of God."—Romans 12:1–2.

"A worldview is basically the lens through which you interpret the world around you."[190]—Alex McFarland

[Biblical Worldview: The integrating of biblical teaching in a person's attitude, standards, ambitions, values, opinions, beliefs and lifestyle.]

Less than one percent of the young adult population holds to a biblical worldview. A biblical worldview is believing that absolute moral truth exists; the Bible is completely accurate in all of the principles it teaches; Satan is considered to be a real being or force, not merely symbolic; a person cannot earn his way into Heaven by trying to be good or do good works; Jesus Christ lived a sinless life on earth; and God is the all-knowing, all-powerful Creator of the world who still rules the universe today.[191] This is alarming. As a potter molds clay into a design of his own, the world desires to mold you into its design. How might this effort be thwarted?

In coffee preparation, it's important to strain out what isn't good by using a great filter to obtain superior taste. To live a superior life, the Christian must have an excellent filter to strain untruth from entering the mind, preventing it from corrupting morals and sound doctrine. This filter is the Bible. The believer must develop the habit of seeing that everything he hears, says, does, and allows entry into the mind passes through this Holy Spirit filtration system, lest heresy overcome him. In utilizing this filtration system, the believer will develop and maintain a biblical worldview.

The Apostle Paul offers specific biblical help in filtering out what would be harmful to the believer's life. He states, "Finally, brethren, whatsoever things are true, whatsoever things are honest, whatsoever things are just, whatsoever things are pure, whatsoever things are lovely, whatsoever things are of good report; if there be any virtue, and if there be any praise, think on these things" (Philippians 4:8). Prior to the admission of any thought or deed into your life, ask the following questions.

Is it not only true but also healthy to ponder or pursue?

Is it honorable, worthy of respect?

Is it the right thing to do? Does it mesh with God's Word?

Is it pure and wholesome?

Is it lovely? Does it promote peace or conflict?

Is it virtuous (having moral excellence)?

Is it admirable—that which emphasizes the positive/constructive over the negative/destructive?

Does it bring praise and glory to God?

This specific filter, along with the entire filtration system of the Word of God, will strain the secular worldview from what enters the mind and heart, establishing the believer in untainted Truth.

ASK YOURSELF

What is a biblical worldview?

In what ways does the world seek to mold the believer?

In which of these ways do you find the greatest struggle and why?

How can a believer thwart the effort of the world and develop a biblical worldview?

A good filtering system for the believer is Philippians 4:8. What questions does it suggest you should ask prior to allowance of anything into your life?

Chapter 23 The Gist of Salvation

"Everyone who calls on the name of the LORD will be saved."—Romans 10:13 NLT.

Regarding salvation, there are five specific facts to embrace as truth.

1) Everyone needs to be saved.

A student continuously found himself before the same trial judge for crimes he committed. The judge's patience finally waned, prompting the question to the youth, "Why is it that you cannot keep from doing wrong?"

"Your honor," the student replied, "I guess I was just born wrong." Man was born wrong (sin), resulting in separation from God (Romans 3:23). Jesus Christ alone can reconcile sinful man to Holy God.

2) Everyone can be saved who wants to be.

The good news of the Gospel is that salvation is available to one and all (Romans 10:13). No one is excluded from God's gift of eternal life, regardless of his baggage of sin or darksome past. The famous American evangelist D. L. Moody was preaching when a man stood and said, "I would come, but I cannot come. The ball chained to my feet won't let me."

Moody replied, "Pick up the ball and come." To everyone, Jesus says, "Pick up the ball of sin and bring it with you." "Christ receiveth sinful men—even me with all my sin."

3) Everyone is saved by the cross.

The way some tell it, there are many ways to be saved—by religious works, good life, church membership, baptism—but they are sorely wrong. Man's separation from God due to sin has only one remedy: the death, burial and resurrection of Jesus Christ and one's personal reception of Him as both Lord and Savior (Romans

129

6:23). "For there is none other name under Heaven given among men, whereby we must be saved" (Acts 4:12), and that name is Jesus! Man is saved by Jesus in the expressing of godly sorrow over sin that results in a "turning away" from it (repentance) and a "turning toward" Christ (faith). Godly repentance coupled with faith results in salvation (Acts 20:21).

4) Not everyone who believes he is saved is, in fact, saved.

Satan, as the master deceiver, has caused many to believe they are saved, when in reality they are not. Jesus warns, "Many will say to me in that day, Lord, Lord, have we not prophesied in thy name? and in thy name have cast out devils? and in thy name done many wonderful works? And then will I profess unto them, I never knew you: depart from me, ye that work iniquity" (Matthew 7:22–23).

5) Everyone can know that he is saved.

Knowledge of salvation is not a hope-so, perhaps-so, or guess-so proposition, but a know-so possibility. John states, "He that hath the Son hath life; and he that hath not the Son of God hath not life. These things have I written unto you that believe on the name of the Son of God; that ye may know that ye have eternal life, and that ye may believe on the name of the Son of God" (1 John 5:12–13). A person may emphatically know with a certainty that he is saved. John MacArthur stated that assurance of salvation is "the birthright and privilege of every true believer in Christ."[192]

ASK YOURSELF

Why is salvation a necessity for all?

Are the conditions for salvation different from person to person, church to church, nation to nation? Why or why not?

How is it possible for a person to be religious, yet miss Heaven?

Explain how a person can know if he is genuinely saved or deceptively lost.

Chapter 24   Once Saved, Always Saved?

"Verily, verily, I say unto you, He that heareth my word, and believeth on him that sent me, hath everlasting life, and shall not come into condemnation; but is passed from death unto life."—John 5:24.

A person "born again" into the family of God can never be "unborn" (John 5:24). Jesus' promise of abundant and eternal life to all who repent and believe is certain (John 10:10; Acts 20:21) and trustworthy. Satan may attack and assault the believers' faith, but he can never steal it. He can never undo what God has done in salvation. At the moment of salvation, the believer's name is written with permanent ink in the Lamb's Book of Life, and neither Satan, demons, nor man can erase it (Romans 8:31–39).

Jesus teaches in John 6:37 that all who come to Him in repentance and faith are saved and that they are saved permanently. No one can "lose" his or her salvation. In John 6:39–40, Jesus says He will not lose anyone who is added to the Kingdom by new birth. The Apostle Peter declares that the Christian is "kept by the power of God" unto salvation (1 Peter 1:5). God's omnipotent and supreme power is well able to keep the believer's faith secure.

Jesus declares that His sheep (those who are saved) will "never perish" (John 3:16). "Never" means never. In Philippians 1:6, Paul affirms that God will see through until its completion in Heaven the saving work He initiated in the believer. John 10:28–29 presents the strongest proof for eternal security, stating that a believer cannot be snatched out of the encompassing hand of God.

Christians can and do sin (1 John 2:1) because of the dualistic nature in us—the flesh (carnal) and the spirit (spiritual). These two wrestle each other, competing for dominion throughout the believer's life (Galatians 5:17). It is when the believer yields to the carnal nature that he or she sins, and although divine discipline may come for the rebellious act, the Christian's salvation is never in jeopardy (Romans 8:1). The Apostle Paul experienced this inner struggle like every other Christian (Romans 7:15–25) and discovered that the appetites of the flesh can only be thwarted by walking in the fullness of the Holy Spirit (Romans 8:1–11). To experience the victorious Christian life, believers must repudiate the flesh every day (1 Corinthians 15:31) and surrender again to the controlling influence of the Holy Spirit (Ephesians 5:15–18). In addition, believers must be deliberate in "sowing" to the Spirit (Galatians 6:8) so that they may "reap" the fruit of the Spirit. Sowing to the Spirit involves cultivating and implementing lifestyle practices which please the Lord. Paul is clear that a person will reap what is sown (Galatians 6:7).

But be clear about this. Eternal security does not convey a license to sin (Romans 6:15). The person who is genuinely saved both desires to avoid sin and delights in doing so. He or she is crushed deeply upon committing sin. Adrian Rogers stated, "Some people say, 'Well, if I believed in this doctrine, then I'd get saved, and I'd sin all I want to.' Friend, I sin all I want to. I sin more than I want to. I don't want to! When you get saved, you get your 'wanter' fixed. As a matter of fact, you get a brand new wanter."[193] In reality, many who profess to be saved but live contrary to the teaching of the Bible are not truly saved (Matthew 7:22–23) but are merely members of the visible church rather than the invisible church. The Apostle John writes of such people: "They went out from us, but they were not of us; for if they had been of us, they would no doubt have continued with us: but they went out, that they might be made manifest that they were not all of us" (1 John 2:19).

Once Saved, Always Saved?

ASK YOURSELF

Can a person genuinely saved ever lose his salvation?

Upon what Scripture do you base this answer?

Does the doctrine of eternal security grant a license to sin to the Christian? Why or why not?

What two natures fight for the control of the believer's life?

What might be the cause(s) of one who is genuinely saved doubting his salvation?

Do you possess eternal security?

135

Chapter 25 Why Students Walk Away from Christ

"Then said Jesus to the twelve, Will you also go away?"—
John 6:67 AKJV.

Why do students walk away from Jesus? It would appear
that once students were introduced to Jesus who could forgive their
sin, erase their past, heal their hurts, save from Hell, and supply
their every need, they would jump at the opportunity to know Him.
Sadly, this is not always the case. Understanding why friends reject
Christ enables you to specifically target those reasons, revealing
their fallacy or futility and providing the opportunity of winning the
friends to Christ.

Some Walk Away Due to Perplexity

A fourteen-year-old student was saved following my simple
presentation of the Gospel. He said afterwards, "That was simple. I
just needed someone to explain it to me." I believe many students
would be saved if presented with the Gospel in simplicity.

Some Walk Away Due to Pleasures

This was the reason for the rich young ruler's rejection of
Christ (Matthew 19:22). In response to my inquiry why he wasn't a
Christian, a student answered, "I guess I love sin too much." Some
students love their drugs, alcohol, gambling, pornography, and
party lifestyle too much to be saved. But Jesus warns, "What shall it
profit a man, if he shall gain the whole world, and lose his own
soul?" (Mark 8:36).

Some Walk Away Due to Pride

Humility, which leads to the bowing of the knee to Christ in
confession of sin, is essential to salvation. Sadly, egotism and a
haughty spirit keep many from taking this step to follow Christ. To
come to Christ, the spirit first must be broken under the preaching
of the cross.

Some Walk Away Due to Phonies

The hypocritical lifestyles of professing Christians turn students away from Christ. What can be done to remedy this problem? First, as a believer, be sure to walk the walk you talk. Second, point lost friends to focus on Christ, in whom there is no fault, not the phonies.

Some Walk Away Due to Their Peers

Too many students allow others to influence them to a negative response to Christ's invitation to be His disciple. If you are such, consider the claims and invitation of Christ without thought of the reaction of others. Don't let a friend dictate the role of Christ in your life.

Some Walk Away Due to Procrastination

No doubt many students intend on being saved at some point; they ever live delaying this most important decision. To these students, I ask with James, "How do you know what your life will be like tomorrow? Your life is like the morning fog—it's here a little while; then it's gone" (James 4:14 NLT). No man is guaranteed tomorrow. Today you may die, and at death, it matters not how well intentioned you were to be saved. In fact, Satan doesn't care how well intentioned a person is in being saved, as long as he remains unsaved. The only sure time for salvation is this moment; rush into His presence in repentance and faith now. "Indeed, the 'right time' is now. Today is the day of salvation" (2 Corinthians 6:2 NLT).

Of all people, the Christian, having tasted that the Lord is good, surely will not walk away from Him. C. H. Spurgeon surmises, "Can you so much as dream of a better friend than He has been to you? Then change not the old and tried for new and false. As for the present, can that compel you to leave Christ? When we are hard beset with this world or with the severer trials within the church, we find it a most blessed thing to pillow our heads upon the bosom of our Savior. This is the joy we have today that we are saved in Him; and if this joy be satisfying, wherefore should we think of changing? Who barters gold for dross? We will not forswear the sun till we find a better light, nor leave our Lord until a brighter lover shall appear; and, since this can never be, we will hold Him with a grasp immortal and bind His name as a seal upon our arm. As for the future, can you suggest anything which can arise that shall render it necessary for you to mutiny or desert the old flag to serve under another captain? We think not."[194] The Christian, in being tempted to leave Jesus, declares with Peter, "Lord, to whom shall we go? thou hast the words of eternal life…[W]e believe and are sure that thou art that Christ, the Son of the living God" (John 6:68–69).

ASK YOURSELF

Which reason cited, in your opinion, is the greatest as to why students walk away from Christ?

How might it be shown futile?

What is the danger in delaying a decision for Christ?

What will a person miss by walking away from Christ?

How might you help a friend who is walking away from Christ to come to Him?

Are you presently walking away from Christ, and if so, why?

Chapter 26 Why Acknowledge God?

"Remember now thy Creator in the days of thy youth, while the evil days come not."—Ecclesiastes 12:1.

Solomon frankly states the grave danger that students will forget God; thus, he strongly admonishes them to remember Him. Why should a student like you remember God?

Because without God, Life Is Empty

The entire book of Ecclesiastes is devoted to an empty man's search for significance and meaning in life; that person is Solomon. Despite his work and acquisition of wine, women and wealth, no relief came to the restlessness in his soul (Ecclesiastes 2:10–11) until he discovered that the real source of meaning in life was not found in stuff, but in God. Pleasures and possessions, good or bad, will not give the soul what only God can.

Because It Will Prevent the Ruinous Effects of Sin

Apart from God, Hell is the limit as to what is possible for a man to do! God alone can preserve a person from wickedness and its inescapable and heartbreaking consequences (Galatians 6:7).

Because of the Influence over Others

Acceptance or rejection of Christ's lordship impacts the lives of friends and classmates. To use influence in its best sense, be a devoted follower of Christ.

Because This Part of Life Has a Purpose

Your life can never be all it should be if you delay personal salvation. Regardless of whatever you may become or do for God twenty or thirty years from now, it will never make up for what He purposed for you to do at this point and time in life. Remember God now, for as youth fades, so will specific, once-in-a-lifetime opportunities of service.

Because Delay Hardens the Heart

Failure to remember God now lessens the likelihood of remembering Him later. In fact, eighty-five percent of students not saved at age eighteen will not be saved. As time passes and the Word goes unheeded, the heart hardens to its need of God.

Because of the Uncertainty of Life

No one has a guarantee of tomorrow. David is correct in stating, "There is but a step between me and death" (1 Samuel 20:3). Life is a frail thread that can snap at any time for every man. Prepare for this certain, yet uncertain, step of death by remembering Christ now as your personal Lord and Savior.

Because of the Reality of Eternity

There is a Heaven to gain and a Hell to shun. There are rewards to reap and great sorrows to escape. All hinges upon one's decision regarding Jesus Christ as personal Lord and Savior and devotion to Him or not.

ASK YOURSELF

Which of the seven reasons stated for remembering God resonates the most with you? Why?

In light of the truth shared, what decision ought you to make for Christ here and now?

For what reason(s) do you think students reject Christ?

How might the sharing of this reading enable friends to remember God sooner rather than later?

Chapter 27 The Countdown to Judgment

"It is appointed unto men once to die, but after this the judgment."—Hebrews 9:27.

In the book *101 Things to Do before You Die,* the author fails to address the most needful thing a person needs to do prior to death—repent of sin and, in faith, trust Christ as Lord and Savior.

The clock is a constant reminder of the rapid passing of one's life. Suddenly it will stop, and you will then enter the eternal domain of Heaven or Hell. Should it stop while you are reading this, where would you go?

Death is a certainty. You *are* going to die. Morticians attest to this fact. Cemeteries and crematories testify to its reality. The Holy Bible affirms it: "It is appointed unto men once to die, but after this the judgment" (Hebrews 9:27). Mark it down. Everyone who has a birthday has a "death-day." We are all terminal. Every town has its cemetery street. A friendly undertaker in Washington, D.C., closes all his correspondence with "Eventually yours."

Next to death's certainty looms its uncertainty. The when, where and how of death is unknown.

Uncertain in How You Will Meet Death

Will you meet death by an automobile or hunting accident, plane crash, heart attack, violent crime, drug overdose, or robbery? These are common ways people die, but there are numerous others we have never imagined, as detailed in the docufiction *1000 Ways to Die*. The plain fact is that you do not know how you will meet death.

Uncertain in Where You Will Meet Death

Will you encounter death at work, school, athletic field, restaurant, church, vacation resort? The question is unanswerable, for the place of death yet is hidden. It could be in the very place where you are reading this.

Uncertain in When You Will Meet Death

The Death Clock is ticking. How many more years, months, weeks, days, hours or minutes yet remain for you? Many who presumed plenty of time to live have been caught off guard and unprepared upon death's unannounced arrival. Age, good health, exercise, diet, great genes and carefulness do not guarantee one will live unto tomorrow.

Death often comes suddenly when a person is least expecting it. The probability of sudden death is not as far-fetched as you may think. Someone dies every two seconds. Almost all people know of someone who met death suddenly and without warning. If you met with sudden death NOW, would you be ready?

Death

You can't escape it, avoid it, cheat it, or buy your way out of it. You can only prepare for it. Knowing the certainty of death and its uncertainty as to the how, where and when, the sensible thing to do is to prepare for it NOW. Tomorrow may be too late; an hour from now may be too late. Now is the only time you may have to prepare for this step into eternity. "Now is the accepted time; behold, now is the day of salvation" (2 Corinthians 6:2).

How to Prepare for Death and Eternity

Acknowledge God

God, the Creator and Sustainer of all, loves you and desires a personal relationship with you through His Son, the Lord Jesus Christ. In knowing God personally, you prepare for life and death. "For God so loved the world, that He gave His only begotten Son, that whosoever believeth in Him should not perish, but have everlasting life" (John 3:16).

146

Admit Sin

Sin (disobedience to God) has hindered this personal relationship and must be removed so you may be reconciled (made right) with God. Agree with God's diagnosis of your condition (separation from Him due to sin) and be willing to have it remedied. The Bible says, "All have sinned, and come short of the glory of God," and, "The wages of sin is death; but the gift of God is eternal life through Jesus Christ our Lord" (Romans 3:23; 6:23).

Accept Christ

Admission of sin is not enough. It must be cleansed from the heart. How? Not by anything you have done or may do (not baptism, religious work, goodness, or church attendance). What you cannot do for yourself, God makes possible through His Son, the Lord Jesus Christ. "For when we were yet without strength, in due time Christ died for the ungodly" (Romans 5:6). "The blood of Jesus Christ, his son cleanseth us from all sin" (1 John 1:7). "I am the way, the truth, and the life: no man cometh unto the Father, but by me" (John 14:6). "For whosoever shall call upon the name of the Lord shall be saved" (Romans 10:13).

Jesus died upon the cross and was raised from the dead to make possible divine forgiveness. Jesus is man's only bridge (Mediator) into the presence of God. He alone reconciles man with God, enabling a personal relationship instantly to take place. "For there is one God, and one mediator between God and men, the man Christ Jesus; who gave himself a ransom for all, to be testified in due time" (1 Timothy 2:4–5).

Act Now

David, when fleeing from King Saul, said to Jonathan, "There is but a step between me and death" (1 Samuel 20:3). In all truthfulness, this may be said by every man. We lift our foot up in apparent health presently, but when it comes down, it may meet death. The step of death—when, where and how will you take it?

Be ready constantly for it by placing faith in the Lord Jesus Christ as Lord and Savior.

My friend, will you at this moment receive God's gracious gift of forgiveness of sin and promise of Heaven at death by inviting Christ Jesus into your life as Lord and Savior? Own up to acts of disobedience and rebellion toward God, asking His forgiveness with a sincere and repentant (change of mind) heart (Acts 20:21). Right now, pray using your own words, or, if preferred, the following prayer, and accept God's gracious invitation of eternal life. It is not the prayer that will save you, but He who hears it.

"God, I am guilty of breaking Your commandments and living apart from authoritative submission to Your Word and Will. I realize that while my sin is inexcusable, it is forgivable through the death, burial and resurrection of Your Son Jesus Christ. Jesus, I invite you into my heart as Lord and Savior to reign as unrivaled King of Kings and Lord of Lords. I turn my back on yesterday to live anew for You. In Jesus' name I do pray. Amen."

ASK YOURSELF

What must a person do to be ready for the certain step of death?

If you were to die within the next five minutes, would all be well between God and you?

Did you pray the prayer on the previous page (or one similar), trusting Christ as Lord and Savior?

Explain the meaning of and make personal application of David's words to Jonathan.

Chapter 28   A Bible Christian

"His delight is in the law of the LORD; and in his law doth he meditate day and night."—Psalm 1:2.

In a day when 4 of 5 Americans state that they are Christians, confusion obviously abounds about who a Christian is, based upon God's Word. Psalm 1 simply and concisely identifies the traits of those who are Bible Christians.

A Bible Christian Is Saved

"He shall be like a tree planted by the rivers of water." Like a tree that is transplanted into new soil (new environment), the Bible Christian has been transplanted from being a slave to sin to being a son of God by the new birth. This is the foundational identification mark of the Bible Christian—one who has been reconciled (set right) to God through repentance and faith in Jesus Christ (Acts 20:21).

A Bible Christian Is Separate

"Walketh not in the counsel of the ungodly, nor standeth in the way of sinners." He is separate from the counsel of the ungodly, the evil principles by which they live and induce him to live, and seeks counsel, advice on the issues of life, from godly men. Not only is he separated from their counsel, but their conduct. In an hour when eighty percent of "Christian" teens state there is no difference in how they live compared to their lost counterparts, the words of the apostle Paul need to be heeded: "Come out from among them, and be ye separate, saith the Lord" (2 Corinthians 6:17). Christians are different from the world.

A Bible Christian Is Sound

"Nor sitteth in the seat of the scornful." I render this text in this fashion: "He refuses to sit in the 'chair' of the atheist or humanist whose purpose is to destroy the believer's faith by sowing seeds of suspicion regarding the existence of God and the creditabil-

151

ity of the Scripture." Wisely, the Bible Christian avoids the classroom and venue where such are "seated." The Bible Christian embraces the words of Paul to young Timothy: "Hold fast the form of sound words" (2 Tim 1:13).

A Bible Christian Is Studious

"In his law doth he meditate day and night." A key identifying mark of the genuine believer is hunger for the Word of God; he "soaks in, digests, absorbs" (meditates) Scripture "day and night," making application of its truths. One meaning of the word "meditate" is "growl"; have you ever growled to know God's Word better?

A Bible Christian Is Steadfast

"Like a tree planted by the rivers of waters," he will not be moved, as the old song says. His constancy is "day and night"—constant in his walk before God and with God; consistent today, but also tomorrow. He starts the day in the Word and then closes the day with it. He is not cold and hot, in and out, up and down; but uniform, constant, stable in His walk with God.

A Bible Christian Is Successful

He "bringeth forth his fruit in his season; his leaf also shall not wither; and whatsoever he doeth shall prosper." He bears fruit "in his season," in God's timing. What a promise to claim! Not seeing fruit from your labor yet? It's not "fruit season." Harvest time is coming; you will reap if you faint not (Galatians 6:9). Success awaits in the work God has commissioned. The genuine Christian will bear fruit (John 15:5)!

A Bible Christian Is Satisfied

"Blessed is the man." The Bible Christian is "blessed" (happy). Happy, happy is the man that walks with the Lord. The Christian walk is not dull or drab, but delightful and joyous, even in the midst of life's difficulties. "Oh, happy day that fixed my choice on thee my Savior and my God."

ASK YOURSELF

In contrasting the traits of a Bible Christian to your life, which do you find most and least similar?

The first trait cited is the *root* of salvation (the remaining traits are the *fruits* of salvation). What is it and how is it obtained?

Based upon this description of an authentic Christian, can you honestly state that you are one?

If not, will you now make a sincere commitment of your life to Jesus Christ, receiving Him as Lord and Savior of your life?

If you are a Christian, which of the "fruit" traits do you need to cultivate and apply more earnestly?

Endnotes

[1] Alex McFarland. *10 Answers for Skeptics* (Ventura, California: Regal Books, 2011), 75.

[2] John Leland, cited in Josh McDowell and Bob Hosteller. *Beyond Belief to Convictions* (Carol Stream, Illinois: Tyndale, 2002), 9.

[3] William Lane Craig. *Reasonable Faith* (Wheaton, Illinois: Crossway Books, 1994), 38.

[4] W. Poole Balfern (1858). Cited in Livingwaters.com Newsletter, October 31, 2011.

[5] Josh McDowell. *Beyond Belief to Convictions*, 26.

[6] Christian Youth Are Leaving the Church. CrossExamined.org, accessed October 26, 2011.

[7] The Committee on Evangelical Unity in the Gospel, Press Statement, June 1, 1999 (The Ankerberg Theological Research Institute)

[8] Clark Pinnock, cited by www.defendingyourfaith.org/Apologetics.htm, accessed May 20, 2011.

[9] Paul Little, cited by www.defendingyourfaith.org/Apologetics.htm, accessed May 20, 2011.

[10] Alex McFarland. *10 Answers for Skeptics*, 141.

[11] Ibid.

[12] William Lane Craig. *Reasonable Faith,* 125.

[13] Alex McFarland. *10 Answers for Skeptics*, 19.

[14] William Lane Craig. *Reasonable Faith,* 125.

[15] J. C. Ryle. "Fire! Fire!" http://www.biblebb.com/files/ryle/fire_fire.htm, accessed December 26, 2011.

[16] "Church of the Non-Believers" Wired Magazine, November 2006. See http://www.wired.com/wired/archive/14.11/atheism.html for the full article.

[17] Youtube. "The New Atheist Movement," accessed March 21, 2011.

[18] Peter Kreeft. *The Reasons to Believe.* www.catholiceducation.com, accessed March 25, 2011.

[19] GodEvidence.com, accessed March 25, 2011.

[20] Rich Deem. *The Incredible Design of the Earth and Our Solar System.* www.godandscience.org/apologetics/atheismintro2.html, accessed March 23, 2011.

[21] Richard Feynman, *The Meaning of It All: Thoughts of a Citizen-Scientist* (New York: BasicBooks, 1998), 43.

[22] Hugh Davson, *Physiology of the Eye,* 5th ed. (New York: McGraw Hill, 1991)

[23] *What does it mean that we are fearfully and wonderfully made (Psalm 139:14)?* gotquestions.org, accessed March 26, 2011.

[24] Phillip Bishop. *Fearfully and Wonderfully Made: Evidence of God in Human Physiology.* OrthodoxyToday.com, accessed March 26, 2011.

[25] Marilyn Adamson. *Is there a God?* EveryStudent.com, accessed March 25, 2011.

[26] Ibid.

Endnotes

---

[27] Carl Cantrell. *Creation, the Science.* http://www.hauns.com/~DCQu4E5g/Complexity.htm, accessed March 25, 2011.

[28] Phillip Bishop. *Fearfully and Wonderfully Made: Evidence of God in Human Physiology.*

[29] *What does it mean that we are fearfully and wonderfully made (Psalm 139:14)?* gotQuestions.org, accessed March 26, 2011.

[30] GodEvidence.com, accessed March 25, 2011.

[31] Ibid.

[32] Sir David Brewster. *Memoirs of the Life, Writings, and Discoveries of Sir Isaac Newton,* Vol. II. (Edinburgh: Thomas Constable and Co., 1855), 347–348.

[33] GodEvidence.com, accessed March 25, 2011.

[34] Phillip E. Johnson, cited in Norman Geisler and Frank Turek. *I Don't Have Enough Faith to Be an Atheist.* (Wheaton, Illinois: Crossway Books, 2004), 1.

[35] C. S. Lewis. *Surprised by Joy* (Orlando, Florida: Harcourt Books, 1955), 227–228.

[36] P. L. Tan. *Encyclopedia of 7700 Illustrations: Signs of the Times.* (Garland, TX: Bible Communications, Inc., 1996). #339.

[37] Alex McFarland. *10 Answers for Skeptics*, 145.

[38] The Always Be Ready Apologetics Blog: New Discovery in Megiddo Mentions Jesus, December 22, 2005.

[39] Flavius Josephus. *Antiquities*, xviii, 33. http://en.wikipedia.org/wiki/Josephus_on_Jesus, accessed May 31, 2011.

[40] Gary R. Habermas, "Was Jesus Real?" InterVarsity.org, August 8, 2008, http://www.intervarsity.org/studentsoul/item/was-jesus-real.

[41] Alex McFarland. *10 Answers for Skeptics*, 194.

[42] The Always Be Ready Apologetics Blog: New Discovery in Megiddo Mentions Jesus. December 22, 2005.

[43] Josh McDowell. "Evidence for the Resurrection." http://www.leaderu.com/everystudent/easter/articles/josh2.html, accessed June 2, 2011.

[44] Michael Green, cited in Lee Strobel. *The Case for the Real Jesus.* (Grand Rapids: Zondervan, 2007), 276.

[45] Lee Strobel. *The Case for the Real Jesus*, 115–116.

[46] Michael Licona, cited in Lee Strobel. *The Case for the Real Jesus*, 122.

[47] Ibid.

[48] Thinkexist Quotations. thinkexist.com/...is_no_mere_book...living_creature/334083.html, accessed October 18, 2011.

[49] Shelton L. Smith, Ed. *Great Preaching on the Bible.* (Murfreesboro, Tennessee: Sword of the Lord Publishers, 2004), 23.

[50] W. A. Criswell, *The Criswell Study Bible* (Nashville: Thomas Nelson Publishing Company, 1979), 1459.

Endnotes

[51] "Archaeology and the Bible." Christiananswers.net/archaeology, accessed December 27, 2010.

[52] Ibid.

[53] Ibid.

[54] Ibid.

[55] "Facing the Challenge." www.facingthechallenge.org, accessed December 22, 2010.

[56] Waine-Ann McLaughlin. "How Archaeology Proves the Bible." www.prevailmagazine.org, accessed December 27, 2010.

[57] Keith N. Schoville. "Top Ten Archaeological Discoveries of the Twentieth Century Relating to the Biblical World." biblicalstudies.info/top10/schoville, accessed October 10, 2011.

[58] Shelton Smith. *Great Preaching on the Bible*, 24.

[59] *Proof the Bible Is Genuine, Authentic, Inspired Revelation of God.* www.choice-s.com/authenticity.htm, accessed March 26, 2011.

[60] Charles C. Ryrie, *The Ryrie Study Bible* (Chicago: Moody Press, 1994), 1991.

[61] Josh McDowell. *The New Evidence that Demands a Verdict* (Nashville, Tennessee: Thomas Nelson, 1999), 9.

[62] Ibid.

[63] John MacArthur. "What Jesus' Death Meant to Him" (August 1, 1971). Gty.org, accessed June 14, 2011.

---

[64] William Fay. *Share Jesus without Fear.* (Nashville: Broadman and Holman Publishers, 1999), 89.

[65] Norman Geisler, cited in Lee Strobel. *The Case for the Real Jesus*, 223.

[66] Josh McDowell. *The New Evidence that Demands a Verdict,* 193.

[67] Shelton Smith. *Great Preaching on the Bible,* 63–64.

[68] Curtis Hutson, cited in Shelton Smith. *Great Preaching on the Bible,* 206.

[69] Alex McFarland. *10 Answers for Skeptics*, 49.

[70] Shelton Smith. *Great Preaching on the Bible,* 127.

[71] Ibid., 131.

[72] Ibid.

[73] 101 Scientific Facts and Foreknowledge. http://www.eternal-productions.org/101science.html, accessed October 8, 2011.

[74] Shelton Smith. *Great Preaching on the Bible,* 133.

[75] Ibid.

[76] Ibid.

[77] Ibid.

[78] Ibid.

[79] Ibid.

[80] Ibid.

[81] Ibid., 80–81.

Endnotes

[82] John MacArthur. *Why Believe the Bible?* (Ventura, California: Regal, 1980), 36.

[83] Ibid., 35.

[84] John Stott. "Teacher and Lord." (Minneapolis: Decision Magazine, March 1961).

[85] Larry Wilson. Daily Devotional. January 23, 2011. www.opc.org/devotional.html?devotion, accessed June 17, 2011.

[86] Cited by Fritz Ridenour. *Who Says.* (Ventura, California: G/L Publications, Regal Books, 1967).

[87] Ravi Zacharias. *Apologetics 315*, June 14, 2009. apologetics315.blogspot.com, accessed March 29, 2011.

[88] This entry is based largely upon Josh McDowell and Don Stewart. "Why Does God Allow Evil to Exist?" in *Answers to Tough Questions Skeptics Ask About the Christian Faith.* (Carol Stream, Illinois: Tyndale, 1980).

[89] John Calvin, cited by John MacArthur. "Is God Responsible for Evil?" (Code: QA134). www.gty.org, accessed March 28, 2011.

[90] John MacArthur. "Is God Responsible for Evil?" accessed March 28, 2011.

[91] Adrian Rogers. "Why Doesn't God Obliterate Evil?" (Devotionals by Love Worth Finding, February 3, 2010). oneplace.com, accessed March 29, 2011. [See "Did God Create Evil?" by Rogers on youtube.com for additional insight on the origination of evil]

[92] Adrian Rogers, "Why I Reject Evolution." sermoncentral.com, accessed March 29, 2011.

[93] Ibid.

[94] Ibid.

[95] Ibid.

[96] Ibid.

[97] Ibid.

[98] en.wikipedia.org/wiki/Science, accessed April 4, 2011.

[99] Henry Morris. "Evolution Is Religion, Not Science." www.icr.org/article/evolution-religion-not-science, accessed April 4, 2011.

[100] John MacArthur. "Evolution: Science or Faith," August 29, 1999. www.gty.org, accessed May 24, 2011.

[101] Josh McDowell. *What's Wrong with Evolution?* http://joshmcdowell.blogspot.com, Wednesday, July 16, 2008, accessed March 29, 2011.

[102] Dr. Kent Hovind, cited by AllaboutGod.net, accessed April 3, 2011.

[103] Ibid. [cited are only a few of the 15 questions Hovind poses]

[104] Ken Ham. *The Answers Book 3*. (Green Forest, Arizona: Master Books, 2010), 301.

[105] Paul Ackerman, cited in John MacArthur. "Creation Day 3," (May 16, 1999). www.gty.org, accessed May 24, 2011.

[106] Frank Barna. *Third Millennium Teens.* (Barna Research Group, 1999).

[107] Josh McDowell and Bob Hosteller. *Belief Beyond Convictions,* 9.

Endnotes

---

[108] Peter Kreeft. "The Uniqueness of Christianity." www.peterkreeft.com/topics.../christianity-uniqueness.htm, accessed June 7, 2011.

[109] Josh McDowell. *Evidence Growth Guide.* (San Bernardino, CA: Here's Life Publishers, 1981), 22–23.

[110] Charles Ryrie. *The Ryrie Study Bible,* 1991.

[111] John MacArthur, *Truth Matters* (Nashville: Nelson Publishers, 2004), 71.

[112] A. W. Tozer, cited in www.sermonillustrations.com/a-z/h/hell.htm, accessed August 16, 2011.

[113] Shelton Smith, "Firestorm Erupts Over Pastor's View of Hell!" *The Sword of the Lord* (Murfreesboro: Sword of the Lord, April 15, 2011), 1.

[114] John Blanchard, *Whatever Happened to Hell?* (Evangelical Press, 2005), 154.

[115] Adrian Rogers. "Five Minutes After Death." www.sermonsearch.com, accessed June 5, 2011.

[116] Leighton Ford. *Good News Is for Sharing.* (Colorado Springs: David C. Cook Publishing Co., 1977), 34.

[117] C. S. Lewis, cited in "Hell—Tough Questions Answered." toughquestionsanswered.wordpress.com/category/hell/, accessed April 6, 2011.

[118] J. I. Packer. *Evangelical Affirmations.* (Grand Rapids: Zondervan, 1990), 123–24

[119] John Ankerberg and John Weldon, "Response to J. I. Packer." www.ccel.us/EV.ch4a.html, accessed April 14, 2011

[120] W. A. Criswell and Paige Patterson, *Heaven.* (Grand Rapids: Tyndale House Publishers, 1991), 121.

[121] *Crossroads.* Issue 7, p. 16.

[122] Jon Courson. *Jon Courson's Application Commentary.* (Nashville: Thomas Nelson, 2003), 555.

[123] Paul E. Little. *Know What You Believe.* (Wheaton: Victor Books, 1979), 189.

[124] Jon Courson. *Jon Courson's Application Commentary*, 556.

[125] W. A. Criswell and Paige Patterson. *Heaven*, 34.

[126] Ibid., 42.

[127] C. H. Spurgeon. *Morning and Evening*, October 10. (Peabody, MA: Hendrickson Publishers, 1991).

[128] Matthew Henry. *Matthew Henry's Commentary on the Whole Bible,* John 14:2. (Peabody, MA: Hendrickson Publishers, 2008).

[129] Jonathan Edwards. "Many Mansions." www.biblebb.com/files/edwards/JE-mansions.htm, accessed April 21, 2011.

[130] Herschel Ford. *Simple Sermons on Heaven, Hell, and Judgment.* (Grand Rapids: Zondervan, 1969), 26.

[131] Randy Alcorn. "Questions and Answers about Heaven." www.precious-testimonies.com/Exhortations/f-j/heaven.htm, accessed April 21, 2011.

[132] W. A. Criswell and Paige Patterson. *Heaven*, 33.

Endnotes

[133] Curtis Hutson, Ed., *Great Preaching on Heaven.* (Murfreesboro, TN: Sword of the Lord Publishers, 1987), 15.

[134] K. S. Wuest. *Wuest's Word Studies from the Greek New Testament for the English Reader*, Heb 12:1. (Grand Rapids: Eerdmans, 1997).

[135] John MacArthur. "What Will Heaven Be Like?" (Questions and Answers: Code: QA111). gty.org, accessed April 23, 2011.

[136] C. H. Spurgeon. *Morning and Evening*, April 22.

[137] Ibid.

[138] Eliza E. Hewitt, cited in William Kirkpatrick and Henry Gilmour. *Pentecostal Praises.* (Philadelphia, PA: Hall-Mack Company, 1898).

[139] Adrian Rogers. "Who Are the Elect?" Youtube, accessed Sept 5, 2010.

[140] Adrian Rogers. *The Passion of Christ and the Purpose of Life.* (Wheaton: Crossway Books, 2005), 67.

[141] Bruce R. Cole. cited in *The Baptist Banner*, September, 2011, p. 18.

[142] Alex McFarland. *10 Answers for Skeptics*, 201.

[143] Norman L. Geisler. *Baker Encyclopedia of Christian Apologetics.* (Grand Rapids: Baker Academic, 1998), 731–732.

[144] John MacArthur. "Our Triune God." gty.org, accessed August 17, 2011.

[145] Norman L. Geisler. *Baker Encyclopedia of Christian Apologetics*, 735.

[146] Ibid.

[147] P. P. Enns. *The Moody Handbook of Theology.* (Chicago: Moody Press, 1997), 200.

[148] C. S. Lewis. Mere Christianity (New York: HarperCollins, 2001), 165.

[149] The Trinity. www.concernedchristians.com/index.php?option, accessed April 5, 2011.

[150] W. A. Criswell. "The Unfathomable Mystery of God," March 1, 1981, The W. A. Criswell Sermon Library. www.wacriswell.org, accessed August 17, 2011.

[151] Norman Geisler. *Systematic Theology*, Vol. 2 (Minneapolis: Bethany House, 2003), 279.

[152] C. S. Lewis. *The Screwtape Letters.* (New York: Macmillian, 1961), 3.

[153] W. A. Criswell. "Satan," March 16, 1958. wacriswell.com, accessed May 19, 2011.

[154] Donald Grey Barnhouse. *The Invisible War.* (Grand Rapids: Zondervan Publishing House, 1965), 30.

[155] C. S. Lewis. *The Screwtape Letters,* 39–40.

[156] Jack R. Taylor. *Victory over the Devil.* (Nashville: Broadman Press, 1973), 9.

[157] Josh McDowell. Josh McDowell Blog, February 11, 2008. joshmcdowell.blogspot.com, accessed May 04, 2011.

[158] Ibid.

[159] *Stand Firm,* May, 2011. (Nashville: Lifeway), 35.

[160] Josh McDowell, cited in "Abide in Christ." www.abideinchrist.com/selah/nov6.html, accessed May 4, 2011.

Endnotes

[161] Adrian Rogers. *Ten Secrets for a Successful Family.* (Wheaton, Illinois: Crossway Books, 1996), 17–18.

[162] C. H. Spurgeon. *Treasury of David,* Psalm 119. www.theresurgence.com, accessed May 30, 2011.

[163] *Calvin's New Testament Commentaries,* Vol. 10, p. 330.

[164] John Piper. *Jesus, the Only Way to God.* (Grand Rapids: Baker Books, 2010), 23.

[165] Adrian Rogers. "Is Salvation in Jesus Christ the Only Way to Heaven?" September 18, 2006. lwf.org, accessed June 13, 2011.

[166] The Committee on Evangelical Unity in the Gospel, Press Statement, June 1, 1999.

[167] P. L. Tan. *Encyclopedia of 7700 Illustrations: Signs of the Times.*

[168] Rogers, "Is Salvation in Jesus Christ the Only Way to Heaven?"

[169] John Stott. The Message of Romans (The Bible Speaks Today series: Leicester: IVP, 1994), 268.

[170] P. L. Tan. *Encyclopedia of 7700 Illustrations: Signs of the Times.* #5406.

[171] J. Budziszewski. *How to Stay Christian in College.* (Colorado Springs: NavPress, 2004), 41–43.

[172] Ibid., 43.

[173] W. Barclay, Ed. *The Letter to the Hebrews, The Daily Study Bible Series,* Rev. ed. (Philadelphia: The Westminster Press, 2000), 104.

[174] Adrian Rogers. "No Other Way to Heaven." lwf.org, accessed June 13, 2011.

[175] Robert Mounce. *Themes from Romans.* (Gospel Light Publications, 1981), 12.

[176] R. C. Sproul. *Reason to Believe.* (Grand Rapids: Zondervan, 1982), 50.

[177] Bill Cashion. Personal Correspondence. October 13, 2011.

[178] Ray Pritchard. "What About Those Who Never Hear The Gospel?" April, 1994. www.keepbelieving.com, accessed June 5, 2011. [adaptation made by this author]

[179] William Lane Craig. "Reasonable Faith: How Can Christ Be the Only Way to God?" reasonablefaith.org, accessed June 9, 2011.

[180] C. S. Lewis. *Mere Christianity,* 64.

[181] Bill Cashion. Personal Correspondence.

[182] Dino Pedrone. "Developing an Absolute Belief System," *The Evangelist.* (Tennessee Temple University Publications, January–February, 2003), 3.

[183] John Stott. *The Message of Galatians.* (Downers Grove, Illinois: Inter-Varsity Press, 1968), 137–138.

[184] Adrian Rogers. *Family Survival in an X-Rated World.* (Nashville: B and H Publishers, 2005), 98.

[185] Ibid.

[186] A. W. Tozer, cited in "Cry for Repentance," www.cdye.wordpress.com/tag/a-w-tozer, accessed April 17, 2011.

[187] C. H. Spurgeon. "The Two Effects of The Gospel"—No. 26, May 27, 1855. www.gospelweb.net/SpurgeonSermons/spursermon26.htm, accessed April 20, 2011.

Endnotes

[188] J. Budziszewski. *True Tolerance: Liberalism and the Necessity of Judgment.* (New Brunswick: Transaction Publishers, 2000), 7.

[189] A. W. Tozer, cited in "Cry for Repentance," accessed April 17, 2011.

[190] Alex McFarland. *10 Answers for Skeptics*, 155.

[191] Jennifer Riley. "Survey: Less Than 1 Percent of Young Adults Hold Biblical Worldview." *The Christian Post,* March 10, 2009.

[192] John MacArthur, cited by Donald Whitney. *How I Can Be Sure That I'm a Christian.* (Colorado Springs: NavPress, 1994), Foreword.

[193] Adrian Rogers. "Seven Reasons Why a Saved Person Can't Be Lost." www.lwf.org, accessed March 8, 2011.

[194] C. H. Spurgeon. *Morning and Evening*, October 23.

CPSIA information can be obtained at www.ICGtesting.com
Printed in the USA
LVOW071131010412

275601LV00002B/3/P